SEATTLE MYSTIC
ALFRED M. HUBBARD

SEATTLE MYSTIC
ALFRED M. HUBBARD

INVENTOR, BOOTLEGGER
& PSYCHEDELIC PIONEER

BRAD HOLDEN

Foreword by Don Lattin

THE
History
PRESS

Published by The History Press
Charleston, SC
www.historypress.com

First published 2021

Manufactured in the United States

ISBN 9781467148061

Library of Congress Control Number: 2021937187

Seattle Mystic Alfred M. Hubbard *tells the story of a young Seattle tech wizard who used radio technology to help Northwest bootleggers during Prohibition, then played a key role in introducing LSD to Silicon Valley. This biography of an incredible, eccentric life is truly a mindblower.*

—*Knute Berger, editor, TV host and author of* Pugetopolis: A Mossback Takes on Growth Addicts, Weather Wimps and the Myth of Seattle Nice

———✧———

This is a captivating history of one of America's most colorful characters—Al Hubbard. Holden dives into the larger-than-life history of a man whose past intersects with rumrunning, spy rings, police informants and psychedelics. Brilliantly told, Holden brings Hubbard's enigmatic character to life.

—*Erika Dyck, PhD, professor at the University of Saskatchewan and author of* Psychedelic Psychiatry: LSD from Clinic to Campus

———✧———

An engaging biography about the mysterious Al Hubbard, who helped pioneer psychedelic therapy and is credited by Stan Grof with developing the model of the high-dose inner-directed session to catalyze a mystical experience.

—*Rick Doblin, PhD, founder and executive director of the Multidisciplinary Association for Psychedelic Studies (MAPS)*

———✧———

This is the remarkable story of Captain Al Hubbard—inventor, con man, secret agent, uranium entrepreneur and indefatigable LSD apostle—who saw the light while high on psychedelics in the early 1950s and never looked back.

—*Martin A. Lee, author of* Acid Dreams: The Complete Social History of LSD: The CIA, the Sixties, and Beyond

———✧———

When Brad Holden first stumbled on "Captain" Al Hubbard a few years ago, he found a crafty Seattle rumrunner who'd achieved national celebrity during Prohibition. But Holden soon discovered that Hubbard's second act—as one of the key, hidden figures behind the psychedelic revolution of the 1960s—would prove even more extraordinary. In this groundbreaking attempt to peel back the many layers of myth and mystery that surround Hubbard's early life as a boy genius, bootlegger and spy, Holden lays out the epic life of a uniquely American character, a trickster who danced across the national stage for almost a half century. Holden, a dogged archaeologist of urban artifact and lore, performs an invaluable service by pulling together this compellingly readable introduction to "The Captain"—a man whose late-in-life dream to change the world with psychedelics is still reverberating through the culture today.

—Ken Dornstein, Emmy-winning producer of Long Strange Trip and author of The Boy Who Fell Out of the Sky: A True Story

❦

Through this wildly fascinating story of Al Hubbard, Holden details a huckster, dreamer and iconoclast who prototyped the next generation of eccentric Seattle tech entrepreneurs and lifestyle gurus. But Holden is getting at so much more here: a place, a time, a mentality that has gotten us to where we are today.

—Thomas Kohnstamm, author of Lake City and Do Travel Writers Go to Hell?

CONTENTS

FOREWORD

Seattle historian Brad Holden stumbled across the saga of Captain Al Hubbard while researching the story of Prohibition in the 1920s and 1930s in the Pacific Northwest. My encounter with the legendary captain came through my work as a historian of the psychedelic era of the 1950s and 1960s, when I was researching my trilogy of books, *The Harvard Psychedelic Club*, *Distilled Spirits* and *Changing Our Minds*.

In this fast-paced account, Holden masterfully brings together these two major chapters in the amazing life of this inventor, adventurer, con artist, LSD evangelist and agent of duplicity.

In both eras of Hubbard's life, the Captain reveals himself as the ultimate double-dealer, working both sides in favor of his own self-interest. During Prohibition, he worked for both the rumrunners and the federal agents assigned to take them down. During the '60s, Hubbard was both a crusader for psychedelic spirituality and an agent of shadowy government forces in the "War on Drugs," the longest and least successful war in U.S. history.

I first heard about Hubbard decades ago from Dick Hallgren, an old friend of mine and colleague at the *San Francisco Chronicle*, where we both spent many years working as newspaper reporters. Dick began his journalism career in the late 1950s in Vancouver, British Columbia, when Hubbard was developing a still-popular method of using LSD and other powerful mind-altering drugs as a means for psychological therapy and spiritual insight. The revelations that twenty-one-year-old Dick experienced during his sessions with Hubbard at Vancouver's Hollywood Hospital in 1959 sent this young newsman on a magical mystery tour that would place him in San Francisco for the dawn of the psychedelic '60s.

Dick worked at the *Vancouver Daily Province* with Ben Metcalfe, who wrote a series of articles about Hubbard's work using psychedelic therapy to treat alcoholics. Metcalfe's stories included his own account as a participant/journalist at the hospital, when he found himself "at one with whole galaxies." Dick and Ben had their own nickname for Captain Hubbard: "Doctor Always."

Later, when I was doing interviews for my books, Hubbard's name kept coming up. Stan Grof, another early psychedelic researcher, met Hubbard when Grof was still working in Prague, behind the Iron Curtain. Hubbard was looking for a new supply of LSD and got some from a Czech company that was producing the still-legal drug. "He showed me papers," Grof told me, "from the American and Canadian government stating that he could transport any substances over the border, so I'm sure the CIA was involved."

Another psychedelic pioneer, Jim Fadiman, crossed paths with Hubbard a few years later in what would later be known as Silicon Valley. I've called Jim "the Forrest Gump of the psychedelic '60s" because he kept making cameo appearances at various stops along the long, strange trip. He lived with Richard Alpert, the man who would be Ram Dass, before Alpert got a teaching job at Harvard and became the legendary sidekick to Timothy Leary, the self-claimed "high priest" of the psychedelic movement. Jim's wife, Dorothy Fadiman, dumped her old boyfriend, Ken Kesey, the founder of the acid-fueled Merry Pranksters, to hook up with Jim. Later in the 1960s, Fadiman was a research associate to Myron Stolaroff and Willis Harman, leaders of the early psychedelic and human potential movement on the peninsula south of San Francisco.

Fadiman's most memorable encounter with Hubbard, who also worked with Stolaroff and Harman, took place in Death Valley. Captain Al liked to take potential LSD therapists on psychedelic training sessions down in the desert. After tripping all day out in nature, Hubbard took Fadiman back to his cabin, where they would come down from the acid by drinking 151-proof rum—a toast to Hubbard's bootlegging past.

"Hubbard thought LSD was the greatest thing that ever happened to the human race," Fadiman told me. "He knew the government didn't understand how to use it, but he was always able to get some."

It remains a mystery as to exactly what role Hubbard played—if any—in the efforts by various U.S. intelligence agencies to use LSD as a chemical warfare agent or instrument of "mind control." The Captain appears to have been a bit of a loose cannon as a government agent. But he was more enamored with J. Edgar Hoover than Timothy Leary and did some consulting work in the late 1960s and early 1970s "probing the relationship between drugs and radical politics."

Prohibition—whether against beer and rum in the 1920s or against marijuana and LSD in the 1960s—is never really about the drugs. It's about who is using the drugs and how the government can use its laws as a means of social control. It begins with rising use among a social group outside mainstream society—Irish immigrants drinking in the 1920s, jazz musicians smoking pot in the 1930s, hippies dropping acid in the 1960s or all-night ravers dosing themselves on Ecstasy in the 1980s. Sensationalized media accounts spark a backlash that leads to a government crackdown.

This was the game played by President Richard Nixon in the "War on Drugs" 1960s and by President Ronald Reagan in the "Just Say No" 1980s. The clearest admission of this comes from John Ehrlichman, who served as Nixon's domestic affairs advisor. "Look," he said, "we understood we couldn't make it illegal to be young or poor or black in the United States, but we could criminalize their common pleasure. We understood that drugs were not the health problem we were making them out to be, but it was such a perfect issue…that we couldn't resist."

What I find most enlightening in *Seattle Mystic Alfred M. Hubbard* is the way in which Brad Holden brings together the unfolding of Prohibition in the 1920s and the declaration of the War on Drugs in the 1960s. Both are sagas riddled with hypocrisy and duplicity—the perfect backdrop upon which to understand the life of Alfred Matthew Hubbard.

—Don Lattin
www.donlattin.com
January 24, 2021

PREFACE

I t all started with an old copper moonshine still that I found in the basement of a Capitol Hill estate sale. The discovery of this artifact triggered a fascination with local Prohibition history, which eventually led to the writing of *Seattle Prohibition: Bootleggers, Rumrunners and Graft in the Queen City*. During the preliminary research of that book, a name kept appearing with increasing regularity. It was not a name I was familiar with, but it soon became apparent that this person represented an important part of the overall story that I would soon be documenting. Pushing aside the towering pile of research material, I grabbed my laptop, typed "Alfred M. Hubbard" into the search bar and watched as a number of interesting results popped up on the screen. Clicking on the first result immediately led me down a deep and mysterious rabbit hole. As a historian, this was a good sign, as rabbit holes are usually a strong indication that something interesting has been found. Intrigued, I continued on in my research of this strange figure. This led me down further passageways, followed by others and, before long, I found myself traveling down a mesmerizing maze of tunnels, caves and bottomless pits. The more I learned about him, the more questions I had. Hubbard was, as the old saying goes, "a riddle wrapped in a mystery inside an enigma." I was completely hooked.

As soon as I completed *Seattle Prohibition*, I was frequently asked the question that I'm sure most writers hear: "What is your next book going to be about?" For me, the answer was abundantly and unhesitatingly clear: a biography about Al Hubbard. His story has been briefly covered in a few other publications, but this is the very first book dedicated to telling the complete and definitive story of his life.

With that, I feel it is important to point out a few things. First, as you can probably gather, there are a lot of myths and legends surrounding Hubbard. This book does not shy away from those elements, but for me, it was important to tell Hubbard's story based on what the factual evidence supports. In order to pull this off, I went deep in my research and have done my absolute best to present his story as historically accurately as possible. I made every effort I could to avoid the pitfalls of sensationalizing (a difficult feat when covering a person like this) and instead give an objective account of his life based on what the historical record supports. In doing so, I try to make it very clear in the book whenever I am addressing something that I wasn't able to absolutely substantiate as being true. Don't think for a second, though, that this means the story you are about to read is in any way a dull or boring history lesson. Quite the contrary. Hubbard was arguably one of the more fascinating figures to emerge from the twentieth century, serving several unique roles in each of the decades he was alive and acting as a symbolic bridge between Prohibition and the later War on Drugs.

There are other things I also wanted to achieve with this book. For one, I feel that Hubbard's story has been underrepresented in the local historical record, and I sincerely hope this book will change that. In addition to being a pivotal figure in local Prohibition history, Hubbard also served as the prototype for what would eventually become the "unconventional Seattle tech genius." That's not to say that people such as Bill Gates and Jeff Bezos would never have existed if it weren't for Hubbard, but he was certainly carrying that torch long before the others. In fact, the mysterious invention that he debuted over a century ago was one of Seattle's first forays into the world of innovative technology. And if that isn't convincing enough, I present to you a certain local TV and radio station by the name of KOMO. Hubbard was the one who built it. Therefore, my hope is that Hubbard's name will soon be recognizable for anyone with even a passing interest in Pacific Northwest history.

On a much wider and grander historical scale is, of course, Hubbard's pioneering role in the history of psychedelics. He has often been called the "Johnny Appleseed of LSD," and for good reason. Long before Timothy Leary encouraged an entire generation to "turn on, tune in and drop out" or before Ken Kesey and the Merry Pranksters were driving around the country in a painted school bus, Alfred M. Hubbard had learned to harness the mind-expanding properties of lysergic acid diethylamide for use as an entirely new form of psychotherapy. Not only that, but he introduced the drug to the first and original roster of LSD disciples back in the 1950s, thus earning his lifelong sobriquet. Psychedelic therapy is now enjoying a renaissance, and a whole new generation is rediscovering the principles laid out by Hubbard and his colleagues almost seventy years ago. Because of this, Hubbard's name has been plucked from obscurity and his story is attracting a new round of attention. My hope is that this book helps boost his standing in this very interesting era of American history.

One of Hubbard's psychedelic associates—a California psychiatrist by the name of Oscar Janiger—once remarked that "nothing of substance has ever been written about Al Hubbard, and probably nothing ever should." I have always interpreted that quote as a challenge of sorts, almost like Janiger was double-dog daring someone to complete such an intimidating project. And to that I say, "challenge accepted." I hope you enjoy.

ACKNOWLEDGEMENTS

There are several people who were invaluable in helping me complete this book and to whom I will be eternally grateful for their services and all the information they helped provide. First and foremost, I would like to thank Al Hubbard's granddaughter Brooke Hart. I first reached out to her as soon as my book proposal had been approved, and she was beyond generous in providing me with stories, memories and facts about her famous grandfather that helped me flesh out who he was as a person. We regularly corresponded back and forth during the writing of this book, and in the process, we developed a cherished friendship. I would also like to thank my acquisitions editor, Laurie Krill. She patiently tutored me during the writing of my first book, and her advice once again helped me for this project. Next, I would like to thank Don Lattin for agreeing to write the book's foreword. It was quite the honor to have such an esteemed writer provide the introduction for this book, and I greatly enjoyed our Zoom conversations. This provides a nice segue for my next pair of acknowledgements, Ken Dornstein and Amir Bar-Lev. Ken and Amir are a well-regarded pair of documentary filmmakers whose work includes the acclaimed documentary series about the Grateful Dead, *Long Strange Trip*. They are currently working on a film about Al Hubbard and the history of psychedelic therapy and, through our correspondence, were the ones who put me in touch with Don Lattin. I cannot wait to see their finished work! Next, a big thanks to author and professor Robert Niemi, PhD, who generously provided me with his own notes on Hubbard, which immensely helped me in filling in some much-needed gaps. Likewise, my conversations with Erika Dyck, PhD—a professor at the University of Saskatchewan—were invaluable in helping me with the history of psychedelic therapy in Canada, including the fabled Hollywood Hospital. Lastly, and in no particular order, were the ones who so generously agreed to read my manuscript, offer feedback and even provide blurbs. This roster of noted authors, scholars, friends and historians includes Knute Berger; Lou Olay; Ross Crockford; Rebecca Demarest; Rick Doblin, PhD; Martin A. Lee; and Thomas Kohnstamm.

ACT I

⚬⚬⚬

Let one concentrate all his energies in one single great effort, let him perceive a single truth, even though he be consumed by the sacred fire.
—*Nikola Tesla*

Chapter 1

THE WIZARD OF PORTAGE BAY

arly in the twentieth century, a mysterious youth suddenly appeared in Seattle newspapers boasting of an invention that promised to transform the world. This was the first public glimpse of Alfred M. Hubbard—an enigmatic figure who does not appear in the pages of many history books. That he has managed to escape the gaze of most academic scholars isn't all that surprising given that Hubbard was a complicated person and deciphering the many layers of his mythology poses a difficult challenge. His story tends to be a Gordian knot of fact and fiction, and it's often difficult to discern where truth ends and fable begins. Much of this mystique was sown by Hubbard himself, who was known to preface conversations with: "I'm going to let you in on a secret. Swear that if you tell anyone, you'll tell them not to tell anyone else." As for the invention itself, people are still scratching their heads over it more than a century later. Indeed, much of Hubbard's story presents itself as an exhilarating puzzle composed of a series of unbelievable life events stacked on one another like a cinematic layer cake.

In one of the more sensational legends surrounding Hubbard's life, he often told associates he had been visited by an angel on two separate occasions. During both visits, this glowing apparition reportedly encouraged his scientific endeavors and informed him that his unorthodox ideas would change the future of humanity. The first of these mystical experiences occurred just prior to the big eureka moment leading to his invention. The second angelic vision would appear to him a few decades later, preceding his pivotal role in transforming Western consciousness with a powerful new psychedelic. As was often the case, though, the actual circumstances of Hubbard's life were so unbelievable that any supernatural embellishments are simply not necessary. And while the adventurous scope of his life often resembled that of a Hollywood movie script, the very beginning of his life is one that began in southern impoverishment.

Alfred Matthew Hubbard entered the world on July 24, 1901, in Hardinsburg, Kentucky. His parents, William and Nellie Hubbard, struggled with intermittent unemployment, and the family lived a poverty-stricken existence in their small, rural town. William's employment history included work as a telephone lineman and sometimes as an electrician, both of which almost certainly played an important role in Hubbard's destiny as an inventor. The details surrounding Hubbard's early childhood remain somewhat murky. Some accounts say that he was a "shoeless hillbilly" who never made it past the third grade, while other accounts maintain he possessed at least an eighth-grade education. It was common during this era for young boys to drop out of school in order to obtain employment and financially assist the family. It is unknown if this was the case for Hubbard, though it is certainly plausible given the family's fiscal woes. Later anecdotal evidence pertaining to the nature of Hubbard's relationship with his father would also support this hypothesis. William Hubbard was described as a cruel man with a known drinking problem who had earned himself a sordid reputation in their small Kentucky community. There were rumors of domestic violence, and in later years, there is strong evidence that he attempted to financially exploit his son's technological abilities. In a 1920 newspaper interview, Hubbard reported that he had a high school education, though this has never been verified.

Sometime prior to Hubbard's twelfth birthday, he and his family moved to Washington State so his father could seek better job opportunities. William had two brothers living in the town of Northport, a small ore-mining town just north of Spokane that once held the distinction of being one of the rowdiest mining camps in the West. Records show that William was able to support his family with various labor jobs throughout eastern Washington.

While Hubbard would call Washington State home for the next several decades, his speech never lost traces of his original Kentucky drawl. Physically, he had a husky build, with his most distinguishable trait being the omnipresent twinkle of mischief in his eyes, often accompanied by a sly grin, as though he were perpetually formulating a devilish plan. He had a very outgoing temperament and was always described as a smart and charming extrovert with no shortage of self-confidence. Those who knew him would

always say that he had a "strong personality."
Hubbard was raised Roman Catholic and would
remain a devoted worshiper throughout his life,
though his faith would take a decidedly more
mystical turn in his later years.

A young Hubbard, who was always known
to have a strong affinity for science, once
accompanied his father on a mining job in
the Coeur d'Alene Mountains of Idaho and
found himself developing a fascination with
the machinery being used at the mining
camp. Around the same time, one of his uncles
introduced him to the field of metallurgy,
which, in turn, led him to learn about the newly
discovered properties of radioactivity. "These
experiences applied strongly to my imagination,"

One of the earliest known
photos of Hubbard, circa
1919. *Public domain.*

he would later recall. Likely fueling Hubbard's inherent curiosity was a
childhood filled with wondrous news stories of exciting new technology
from such names as Alexander Graham Bell, Thomas Edison and Henry
Ford. Around the same time, a Serbian-American inventor named Nikola
Tesla was focused on developing technology to transmit electrical power
without the use of wires. Tesla seemed to be a particularly significant
influence, as was evident by the very similar types of technology that
Hubbard was attracted to. The esoteric writings of German engineer Ernst
Leimer, who was a pioneer in the conversion of electricity from radioactive
compounds, also proved to be influential for a young Hubbard after he
discovered one of Leimer's articles in a science magazine.

In Hubbard's early teens, he and his family moved across the Cascade
Mountains, settling among the soggy rainforests, gray skies and craggy inlets
of the Hood Canal region. Hubbard would intermittently call this region
of the Pacific Northwest home for the next fifty years. When Hubbard was
sixteen, his father accepted a job working as an electrician at the Skinner &
Eddy Shipyard in Seattle, prompting yet another family move—this time to
the Puget Sound area. It was here that Hubbard's first angel visit reportedly
occurred, prompting him to quietly begin work on an arcane device that
would soon become national news.

It remains a mystery how, exactly, Hubbard acquired the skills and
knowledge for such technology. Some accounts maintain that he had traveled
to Pittsburgh in his late teens and was able to talk his way into a job with

early radium manufacturer Standard Chemical Company. As the story goes, it was here that he acquired some level of expertise in the then primitive science of atomic energy. After this apprenticeship, Hubbard returned to Washington State and set up a home laboratory in the town of Everett, where he spent all his time, energy and finances working on a generator capable of producing an unlimited supply of power without reliance on any traditional energy sources. Such a machine has long been the goal of scientists going back many centuries. Several of Leonardo da Vinci's famous drawings featured devices capable of making free energy, and even Nikola Tesla claimed to have developed a scientific principle that supported the idea of perpetual motion. With some of the greatest thinkers in human history in search of such technology, Hubbard worked feverishly to construct this holy grail of energy production.

On December 16, 1919, a photo of Hubbard appeared on the front page of the *Seattle Post-Intelligencer*. In the photograph, a slightly grinning Hubbard—attired in an all-black outfit with a strange motif on his shirt—demonstrates his new invention by using it to power a light bulb. He named his machine the "atmospheric power generator." According to the article's astonishing claims, his invention extracted energy from the Earth's atmosphere and then converted it into usable electricity. It was, in essence, a "free energy machine" that Hubbard claimed could then be used to power cars, boats and even planes. When questioned about it in an interview, he gave the Tesla-esque explanation that it "transformed the earth's line of magnetic forces into electrical energy available for use." In another interview, he cited the Idaho mining camp as one of the sources for his inspiration of the invention: "I watched a great belt flit by me day after day," Hubbard recalled, "and I noted, as thousands before me had, that I could draw an electrical spark from the belt with my finger. I had always been interested in electricity and had studied a great deal from books since I was a small boy. The spark of the belt fascinated me. One night I conceived the idea that developed later into the generator. I will not say that it utilizes in any way the current derived by friction as from the belt. That is not accurate. I am not prepared to divulge the nature of the actual translation of energy."

Whatever the impetus, Hubbard's mysterious generator became an immediate news sensation, even receiving some national coverage, with one headline excitedly heralding him a "boy wizard!" This naturally attracted the attention of the science world, many of whom were interested in examining this exciting new technology. Hubbard declined these requests, stating that he needed to protectively safeguard his invention until it had received a

Hubbard demonstrating his generator for the first time and using it to power a light bulb, 1919. *Public domain.*

patent. As one newspaper article explained, "Because he has not yet obtained a patent upon his discovery, young Hubbard is reticent to speak of his instrument or allow outsiders to get more than a glimpse of his apparatus." His one exception to this was Reverend William E. Smith, a professor of physics at Seattle College (now Seattle University). Hubbard reasoned that a science professor who was also a devout religious man would be an especially credible source and approached Reverend Smith about inspecting his device and giving a testimonial about it to the local press. Upon his examination, Smith proclaimed, "I unhesitatingly say that Hubbard's invention is destined to take the place of existing power generators and that within a few years it will have advanced the whole theory and practice of electricity beyond the dreams of present-day scientists."

Despite Reverend Smith's testimony, Hubbard's unusual level of protectiveness over his invention led to widespread suspicion about its scientific legitimacy. Carl Edward Magnusson, dean of the University of

Washington College of Engineering, was quite blunt in his skepticism: "It sounds like trickery to me and I will not venture an opinion until I have seen it." Some even questioned if the whole thing was nothing more than an elaborate hoax. Hubbard didn't exactly do much to quash such rumors when he founded the Hubbard Universal Generator Company. With this new start-up business, Hubbard actively began seeking the donations of local investors and financial backers with the promise that millions of dollars in dividends would be paid back once his device was eventually patented and enjoying commercial success. In April 1920, a local article announced, "A hundred thousand dollar company has been incorporated in Everett to assist Alfred Hubbard, the youthful inventor of an 'atmospheric power generator.'" By the following year, the capital of Hubbard's enterprise was reported to be as high as $5 million.

On July 28, 1920, with public speculation steadily mounting, Hubbard decided to finally hold a live demonstration of his invention by using it to power a boat on Lake Union. The weather that day was overcast though pleasant, with temperatures in the mid-seventies. Word of Hubbard's demonstration had spread fast, and a crowd quickly gathered at the Queen City Yacht Club on Portage Bay to witness this exciting event. Many potential investors, curious about the veracity of his claims, were also in attendance. At the specified time, Hubbard made his appearance, cutting quite the dashing figure in a suit, tie and matching brimmed hat. Walking out to a nearby wharf, Hubbard turned and, with a dash of showmanship, waved to the crowd before stepping into a boat. With an impish grin, he then powered up his atmospheric power generator and used it to launch the eighteen-foot craft out into the water. For many, it was a spectacular display of technological ingenuity that drew an immediate round of applause. In an odd bit of foreshadowing, this lakefront arena would later become the epicenter of a massive technological industry that would dramatically transform the twenty-first century. On this day, though, Seattle was still a humble town with only a modest amount of technological aspiration, so news of Hubbard's invention had drummed up a fair amount of native excitement. Joining him onboard was his father, William, as well as an investor whom they agreed could accompany them. According to various accounts, the demonstration got off to a shaky start when Hubbard had difficulty getting the motor started and had to make frequent stops to prevent the generator from overheating. The boat was eventually able to attain speeds up to ten knots and was out on the lake for over an hour.

Local newspapers heralded the event as a scientific breakthrough. One journalist even pondered the ramifications of Hubbard's device, proposing that it would likely result in the closure of power plants as well as the demise of the oil industry. Despite all the accolades, several local capitalists were left skeptical about what was actually powering the generator, including the investor who had been onboard. Speaking to reporters afterward, the man admitted that the demonstration intrigued his interest but that he would be "holding off for now." An engineer in attendance was less than impressed by Hubbard's boat demonstration, declaring to a reporter, "Attempted perpetual motion. All bosh! Another Keeley motor. He's a faker!"

Despite the dubious rebukes, Hubbard remained upbeat and announced that he would next be using his device to power a car. The following month, an article in the *Seattle Star* confirmed that Hubbard had, indeed, used his generator to power an automobile in Everett, attaining an average speed of twenty-two miles per hour and covering a total distance of sixteen city blocks. Speaking to reporters afterward, Hubbard denied that his device was a perpetual motion machine; rather, he explained, it ran on "cosmic energy," adding, "I have hitched my wires to the tail of the universe, you might say." This would be the last known demonstration of the atmospheric power generator, though Hubbard worked hard to keep his name in the papers with other electronic gadgetry that he was supposedly working on. This included an X-ray machine that used magnetic waves; a device that restored sight to blind people; and a "vision box" that strongly resembled what would eventually become the television set. The fate of these other inventions remains unknown, as they were never substantiated by any witnesses, nor did Hubbard ever seek a patent for any of them.

In autumn of 1920, Hubbard married his first wife, May Cunningham. She was a sixteen-year-old neighbor who lived in the house next to his Everett laboratory and would accompany him for much of his early promotional endeavors. The young couple traveled to New York City, where Hubbard boasted to the local press that his generator was capable of powering an entire house. Hubbard seemed to refocus his efforts on attracting investors for the Hubbard Universal Generator Company, which, by this time, had also been incorporated in Spokane and Everett. Not surprisingly, his father was listed as one of the trustees. Rumors began circulating that local aviation companies were interested in obtaining the rights to his generator. Specifically, it was announced that Hubbard was working directly with the Symons-Russel Aviation Company, an aeronautics enterprise based in Seattle, though there was suspicion that the whole story was being manufactured in order to generate financial excitement among potential investors. Consistent with Hubbard's mysterious manner of operations, his work with the aviation company was reportedly being carried out "behind locked doors."

Despite all the local publicity, as well as the alleged promise of a lucrative contract with a known airplane manufacturer, Hubbard curiously made a sudden move to Pittsburgh in 1921 and began working for the Radium Chemical Company. It was rumored that his hasty departure from Seattle was prompted by angry investors demanding the returns that had been promised to them. According to Hubbard, Radium Chemical Company—which had strange ties to his earlier employer, Standard Chemical Company—had agreed to fund the completion of his power generator in exchange for a majority stake of the device. After only a couple years, though, the two parties suddenly severed ties with each other, and Hubbard returned to Seattle. There is no record that Hubbard ever developed any type of technology for the company, and no patent was ever issued for his device.

Hubbard demonstrates his generator on Seattle's Lake Union. *Public domain.*

After Hubbard's return from the East Coast, his technical services would be sought out by Seattle's top bootlegger and, among their many Prohibition-era adventures together, would welcome the city to one of its earliest radio stations. As for the atmospheric power generator, the truth about what powered it wouldn't be revealed until many decades later.

Chapter 2

BOOTLEGGING AND
THE BIRTH OF SEATTLE RADIO

It was a warm spring afternoon in Seattle—the type of idyllic day where the city's inhabitants slowly emerge from their winter lairs to giddily soak up some badly needed sunshine amid all the newly blooming daffodils, tulips and flowering cherry trees. On this particular day, Hubbard was hard at work inside a new store that he had just opened. While in Pittsburgh, he had developed a strong interest in the emerging field of radio communication after hearing broadcasts from some of the nation's earliest commercial stations. It was a new industry, and transistor radios were slowly becoming a popular household item. Using his tech savvy to stay ahead of an emerging trend, Hubbard decided to open Seattle's first radio supply store where customers could purchase the proper equipment needed to listen to these exciting new programs. The store was located near Colman Dock, on Seattle's waterfront, and, as a harbinger of things to come, was one of the city's first enterprises dedicated solely to selling new technology.

Hubbard spent most of his days in the back of the store, assembling transistor radio sets, as was the case on this fateful spring day when he heard the bell on the front door clang, signaling that someone had just entered his shop. He set his project down and stood up, ready to welcome a potential new customer. A well-dressed and somewhat familiar-looking gentleman stood near the entrance, curiously looking around at the intriguing inventory of transistors, vacuum tubes and assorted radio parts. Greetings were exchanged, and after a round of small talk, the stranger introduced himself as local attorney Jerry Finch. Once supplied with a name, Hubbard was able to make the mental connection of who exactly this man was. Finch was well known in the local papers as the attorney for "King of the Puget Sound Bootleggers" Roy Olmstead. At the time, Prohibition was in full swing, and Olmstead—a former Seattle police officer—had become the region's top liquor boss, supplying all the city's clubs and speakeasies with top-shelf booze that he and his men smuggled down from Canada using custom-built speed boats. Olmstead's exploits were well known throughout the city, where he had become a bit of a folk hero.

Finch explained that Olmstead wanted to meet the young inventor to discuss a job proposal. At the time, Hubbard and his wife were living hand-to-mouth in a cramped apartment as he struggled to get his new business up and running. It was a financially stressful time for the young couple, especially given that his wife was pregnant with their first child and Hubbard was in serious debt to several different creditors. The possibility of a big paycheck, therefore, was very appealing. With the allure of a potential lucrative job offer, Hubbard promptly closed his shop for the day, and the two men set off for the attorney's office at the nearby Smith Tower.

Olmstead had become quite affluent thanks to his bootlegging operation, which had grown to such an enormous degree that, for a time, he was Puget Sound's largest employer. With so much money rolling in, he and his wife, Elise, had recently purchased a posh estate in the Mount Baker neighborhood that became known as the Snow White Palace. The Olmsteads were known for holding lavish parties and parading around town in luxury automobiles. Unfortunately for him, the Federal Prohibition Bureau had recently set up an office in downtown Seattle, and local liquor rackets were starting to feel the heat. Prior to their arrival, the only concern for Seattle's fraternity of bootleggers were the local police, who could easily be paid to look the other way. These new federal agents, however, played by a different set of rules and seemed immune to bribery. As a result, Olmstead was forced to think of other, creative ways in which he could stay a step ahead of the feds.

When the two men arrived at Finch's downtown law office, a very friendly and cordial Olmstead was waiting for them. At the time, Olmstead was thirty-eight years old and enjoying the best years of his life. He was known as "the Gentleman bootlegger," as he didn't allow his men to carry guns or engage in violence, and he avoided other vice such as gambling, narcotics or prostitution. Balding, very well dressed and with a slightly chubby build thanks to all the fine dining he could now afford, Olmstead looked like a typical crime boss from that era, though with a decidedly more genial temperament than many of his underworld peers. His laugh was said to be infectious. Introductions were made, and Olmstead got straight to the point about the reason for this impromptu meeting. He explained that he had been following Hubbard's engineering feats going back to the atmospheric power generator and wanted to offer him a job as a technician. Specifically, Olmstead needed someone who could install communications equipment aboard the fleet of cars, boats and planes used in his bootlegging operation, and to his way of thinking, Hubbard seemed like the right man for the job.

When presented with an opportunity, Hubbard had a natural aptitude for doing a quick round of mental arithmetic in order to calculate how to reap the greatest benefits. With such an important opportunity now sitting in front of him, he took a few minutes to think the situation over and, after a moment of consideration, accepted Olmstead's offer—with some stipulations, of course. First, he would need Olmstead to pay off several thousand dollars of debt he had accrued, as well as open a charge account for his pregnant wife. Additionally, he requested that he and his wife move into the basement of Olmstead's estate. He had read about Olmstead's new home in the papers and knew that he would need such an area for a proper workspace. Not to mention, he desperately wanted out of the tiny apartment that he and his wife had been living in. Lastly, Olmstead would need to advance him any money needed for the job, no questions asked. With a big grin on his face, Olmstead handily agreed to all of Hubbard's terms and even threw in the free and unlimited use of one of his luxury cars. The two men then shook on a deal that would dramatically shape each of their respective destinies in a very profound way.

In no time at all, Hubbard and his wife were enjoying the luxury of living at Olmstead's mansion. Hubbard transformed Olmstead's basement into his own well-stocked electronics laboratory, where he spent his days constructing sophisticated communications gear. The radios aboard Olmstead's rumrunning ships were of particular importance, as they gave his operation some boat-to-shore communication advantages over the constantly prowling Coast Guard. The basement lab was used for other projects as well, including a polonium-tipped spark plug that Hubbard later received an official patent for. Olmstead, in turn, also relied on Hubbard's mechanical skills to maintain the engines for his various vehicles.

Olmstead's wife, Elise, was a vivacious English woman whom the bootlegger originally met while still married to his first wife. Like Hubbard, Elise could be opportunistic and quite persuasive. After dating Olmstead for a few months, she grew tired of being his mistress and soon pressured him to make the necessary changes in his life that would allow them to be together—which he did. They were soon married, and Elise quickly became an influential voice in his bootlegging operation, helping direct many important business decisions that enabled Olmstead to become the region's top liquor kingpin. After the Hubbards moved into their estate, Elise became close friends with Hubbard's wife, and the close physical proximity of the two couples enabled her to observe Hubbard's technical genius firsthand. From this, she formulated another bold plan. The tea leaves at the moment clearly indicated that the feds were slowly moving in on Olmstead's operation and that they would eventually need a legitimate and legal business to fall back on. She also knew, from talking to Hubbard, that the business of radio had enormous potential to be quite profitable. So why not have the young inventor build them their very own radio station? Elise knew that the time was right for such a venture, as they were currently flush with money. Before discussing the plan with anyone else, she first approached Hubbard, who was very enthusiastic about the idea, and with his backing, they were eventually able to convince Olmstead to sign off on the endeavor. Hubbard negotiated a $15,000 fee for the project and immediately set out to build one of the city's first radio stations.

After months of focused work, Hubbard completed his project, and KFQX hit the Seattle airwaves in October 1924. Olmstead ran the radio station, powered by a one-thousand-watt radio tower, from one of his upstairs bedrooms. The station would air nightly broadcasts that mostly consisted of news and weather. Afterward, Elise would air her popular program *Aunt Vivian*, in which her character would read bedtime stories to a dedicated fan base of local children. This led to the popular idea that she was secretly inserting coded messages into these stories in order to assist her husband's bootlegging operation. This has neither been proven nor debunked and, whether true or not, remains a popular urban legend. At some point, Olmstead and Hubbard added another radio tower on the top floor of the Smith Tower, which, at the time, was Seattle's tallest building. Live jazz music was soon added to KFQX's programming lineup, and before long, sponsors were lining up to purchase advertising spots.

Despite all the excitement over the new radio station, Olmstead's primary focus was his bootlegging operation. In later court testimony, Hubbard would claim that he had been unaware of his partner's illegal booze racket and had been naively taken advantage of by the elder kingpin. The truth of the matter is that Olmstead had gradually incorporated an eager-to-learn Hubbard into his smuggling operation, first as an apprentice—teaching him all the ins and outs of the bootlegging trade—and eventually as one of his

Roy and Elise Olmstead during Prohibition. *Courtesy of Museum of Industry and History (MOHAI).*

most trusted lieutenants. Hubbard learned how to place orders with booze suppliers in Canada, as well as how to pick up those orders in Olmstead's smuggling ships. He found that he really enjoyed the excitement that came with this new profession—whether it was the late-night rumrunning excursions that often resulted in high-speed chases by patrolling Coast Guard ships or mingling with the local criminal underworld at one of Olmstead's decadent parties. For a person from such a destitute background, all the glitz and glamour of this new life was an absolute thrill.

While Hubbard was enjoying his nascent orbit in the bootlegging world, Olmstead had developed an acrimonious feud with a local Prohibition official. William Whitney was assistant director and chief enforcer for the local Prohibition Bureau and had diligently spent months trying to infiltrate Olmstead's operation. Much to his dismay, though, he found himself continually running into dead ends as the liquor kingpin's citywide payoff system had made his enterprise virtually impenetrable. Out of sheer frustration, Whitney began wiretapping Olmstead's phone lines. However, this also proved to be a futile endeavor, as Olmstead was tipped off about the eavesdropping and began using his phone conversations to toy with Whitney—setting up fake landing spots for his booze deliveries and just generally playing a series of cat-and-mouse games with the Prohibition director. At some point, it became personal between the two men, their rivalry even spilling into the pages of the local press and putting Whitney's job in jeopardy. With his career now on the line, Whitney realized the only way to bring Olmstead down was with a search warrant and resorted to unscrupulous means to obtain one. By fabricating some of the wiretapping records as well as intimidating witnesses into providing false testimony, Whitney finally got a Seattle judge to sign off on a warrant, thereby giving him the means to conduct a raid and hopefully shut down the city's top bootlegging enterprise once and for all.

On the evening of November 17, 1924, Whitney gathered a small battalion of well-armed government agents and led a caravan of cars over to the Olmstead residence. Upon their arrival, Whitney and his weaponized delegation stormed through the front door and rounded up all the occupants of the house, including Olmstead and Hubbard, who were said to be reading the newspaper funny pages together in the living room. Everyone was ordered into the kitchen and held at gunpoint while the agents began an aggressive search for any incriminating evidence. Even Elise, who was upstairs doing her nightly radio show—as well as the radio engineer who was live producing her show—were forced off the air and ordered to go stand with the others. Olmstead's mansion was completely ransacked, and afterward, everyone was placed under arrest and charged with conspiracy to violate the National Prohibition Act. Whitney and his agents managed to seize assorted business documents and tax records that were enough to later secure a grand jury indictment. The two official charges were cited as "illegal importation of liquor from Canada" and the "illegal distribution and sale of intoxicating liquors." Each individual charge carried a $10,000 fine and up to two years in prison. Olmstead and his crew, including Hubbard, were now looking at the very real possibility of serving some hard time.

Once the charges were made official by a Seattle grand jury, the gravity of the upcoming trial quickly became evident to everyone involved. Known as the "Whispering Wires Case," due to the extensive wiretapping involved, the resulting legal proceeding would end up being the biggest Prohibition trial in history. Olmstead, seemingly unfazed, simply posted bail and returned to work—setting his liquor operation right back into motion again. The trial for these charges wouldn't be for another year, and in the meantime, he had a thirsty city to accommodate. Due to the mounting legal costs associated with the upcoming trial, however, Olmstead decided to sell his radio station, and it fell under the ownership of a local businessman named Birt Fisher, who changed the call sign to KTCL ("Know The Charmed Land") in order to rid it of any association with the illegal liquor trade. Today, that station continues to operate as Seattle's KOMO TV and radio.

Hubbard, meanwhile, had been quite shaken by the whole ordeal, and the fallout from the arrest was proving to be detrimental to his financial status. Olmstead's liquor business had been kneecapped, and the radio station that he had painstakingly built from scratch had been sold, thus ending all the advertising revenue it had once been generating. Also, after a couple years of marriage, Hubbard's wife, May, had filed for divorce on grounds of "neglect" and was now requesting alimony. Worst of all, Hubbard felt like his scientific reputation had been badly tarnished from all the negative publicity. Always the schemer, the young inventor began planning what his strategy was going to be for getting himself out of this mess.

He ultimately decided to become an informant in exchange for having his name dropped from the indictment. He set up a meeting with William Whitney, and during their private conference, Whitney listened intently to Hubbard's proposal, though he remained suspicious about his motives. When asked about this, Hubbard explained how his association with Olmstead had sullied his "scientific reputation," which he now wanted to restore by refocusing his efforts back on radio and electronics. In the end, Whitney was desperate to see the case through to prosecution and agreed to the proposal, knowing that the young inventor had a wealth of inside knowledge regarding Olmstead's operation. After settling on their agreement, Whitney stood up, ready to see his new informant to the door, but Hubbard remained seated. He wasn't quite finished negotiating just yet. In addition to having his name dropped from the indictment, Hubbard also insisted that he be appointed

Roy Olmstead operating radio station KFQX out of his home in 1924. This was one of Seattle's first radio stations that would eventually become KOMO. *Courtesy of MOHAI.*

as a Prohibition agent. Whitney stared back in disbelief. Without question, this was certainly a bold proposal on Hubbard's part and was completely unusual in terms of deals typically offered in such situations. But Whitney was a desperate man and, knowing that Hubbard's testimony would all but ensure a guilty verdict for Olmstead, hesitatingly agreed to Hubbard's proposal. He had some conditions of his own, though. First, Hubbard would work exclusively as an undercover agent embedded in Olmstead's racket and would not have access to any other federal operations. Also, he would be required to provide detailed weekly reports related to his covert assignment. Both men agreed to each other's terms, and the ball was set in motion. As would be later revealed, though, Hubbard had certain other financial motivations in mind with this arrangement.

Hubbard's appointment as an agent was quite unconventional and took a considerable amount of political maneuvering, but with some high-level assistance, the twenty-four-year-old Hubbard was quietly appointed as a Prohibition agent on October 3, 1925. He continued to work as

Elise Olmstead doing her *Aunt Vivian* radio show, 1924. *Courtesy of MOHAI.*

Olmstead's top lieutenant while, unbeknownst to anyone else, he was also having clandestine meetings with the Prohibition Bureau in order to feed them secret bits of information. When it came to the weekly reports that he was required to provide, it quickly became apparent that bureaucratic paperwork was not one of Hubbard's strong points. His reports were often of subpar quality and seldom contained data of any actual value. In addition, Prohibition officials were discovering that Hubbard was hard to pin down and was seldom where he was supposed to be. An increasingly frustrated Whitney would often sit Hubbard down to try and pull specific information from him but found it to be a tedious process, as Hubbard had a knack for changing the topic of conversation to all the various gadgets and inventions he was working on. Other buttoned-down administrators at the Bureau had similar experiences. Hubbard would often wander into random offices and interrupt important work time with impromptu discussions about technology. Whitney described Hubbard as having a "peculiarity of temperament and was rather eccentric," which many at the department attributed to Hubbard's status as an inventor. Whatever the reason, Hubbard's antics were quickly trying everyone's patience. Not only did he struggle with the by-the-book regime of government service, but as time wore on, suspicions started growing about his loyalty as an agent. Hubbard would often provide detailed information regarding Olmstead's business rivals yet would only provide "meager" reports pertaining to Olmstead's operation itself. When confronted about these concerns, Hubbard would always manage to steer the conversation to the topic of radio technology, causing the matter to eventually be dropped out of sheer exasperation. That he represented a guilty verdict against Olmstead is likely the only thing that prevented him from being dismissed as an agent.

Meanwhile, in Hubbard's other life, he had been increasingly drawn to the world of rumrunning and was enjoying his time aboard Olmstead's fleet of ships. At the time, rumrunners in the Pacific Northwest had started taking advantage of nearby Boeing Airfield, with its abundance of fighter planes leftover from World War I, and started using surplus airplane engines to power their boats. This gave their smuggling ships unbelievable power and speed, allowing them to outrun Coast Guard vessels and avoid capture. The skipper of Olmstead's rumrunning ships was a half–Native American adventurer by the name of Prosper Graignic who, for many years, held the boat speed record on Seattle's Lake Washington. Graignic would frequently invite Hubbard to join him on late-night smuggling excursions, often during stormy weather.

Adding to the danger and excitement, the Coast Guard cutters were now aggressively patrolling Puget Sound waters and were not afraid to use machine guns or high-powered cannons on any suspicious boats. For Hubbard, the whole thing was a big thrill. Olmstead even put Hubbard

Hubbard, during his bootlegging phase, holding a pair of binoculars used to spot Coast Guard ships. *Public domain.*

in charge of purchasing new ships, giving him a set of maritime skills that would play a pivotal role in one of his later life chapters. It was during these high seas adventures that Hubbard would meet the woman who would eventually become his second wife and with whom he would spend the rest of his life. Her name was Rita, and they met on a smuggling ship named *Seahawk* on its return from a late-night booze run.

Things took a decided turn for the worse on Thanksgiving Day 1925. Olmstead and his men were unloading a shipment of booze on Woodmont Beach, south of Seattle, when a trio of armed Prohibition agents stepped out of the woods and ordered everyone to put their hands up. Along with Olmstead, the agents arrested everyone who was present, including Hubbard. The agents were completely unaware that Hubbard was a fellow agent or that he had been working undercover, so he was handcuffed along with the others. Whitney was notified of the arrests and immediately drove down. He was jubilant about the news with regard to Olmstead but was less than amused over Hubbard's involvement, who offered the flimsy explanation that Olmstead had sprung the delivery on him at the last minute and so he didn't have time to sneak away and alert anybody. For Whitney, it was further confirmation that Hubbard was working both sides.

Likewise, Olmstead had developed his own suspicions about Hubbard. There was scuttlebutt among the local bootlegging community that Hubbard had been seen with known Prohibition agents, and Olmstead's inner circle was starting to become worried, especially given the upcoming trial. Hubbard was eventually summoned to Jerry Finch's office, where the attorney confronted him about all the rumors and accusations that were swirling around. Hubbard confessed to being an agent but assured Finch that his only motive in becoming an agent was to act as an undercover mole and that, behind the scenes, he was secretly working on Olmstead's behalf. Upon hearing Hubbard's admission, Finch reportedly broke down in tears over the apparent betrayal. With Hubbard's secret now out in the open and both sides suspicious about the other, a meeting was soon set up between Olmstead, Finch and Whitney at the Prohibition office. It was now time for all parties to sit down and discuss the "Hubbard situation."

The official transcript from that conversation reveals a somber conversation, with Olmstead getting straight to the point about matters. "My lawyers are hounding me for a lot of money as I have put up some real coin," he stated. "I have just received some information that leads me to believe that Hubbard is a Prohibition agent. I had heard a rumor sometime back that he was connected with you fellows, but I took him to task about it and he denied it and I kept on trusting him and didn't take any stock in it. But some things have happened here recently that I believe he might be an agent."

After a short pause, Whitney replied, "Well, Roy, the jig is up. Hubbard is an agent, and he absolutely has the goods on you and a lot more others."

Olmstead's mouth fell open, his face became ashen and he said nothing for a few moments. Then, in a husky voice, he exclaimed, "Well I'll be damned. I never would have believed it. That damn scoundrel certainly fooled me good. He's got me in a jam and a lot more of my good friends." After hesitating for a few moments, he simply concluded, "Well, I'm done." Realizing his predicament, Olmstead informed Whitney that he would not be throwing any further money into fighting the charges and sullenly left the meeting, a defeated man.

A month later, the *Seattle Star* published an article revealing Hubbard's role as an agent, describing him as a "shadowy figure who worked both sides of the street." Hubbard's secret was now public knowledge. Oddly, Hubbard continued to work alongside Olmstead, whose liquor business had started to seriously falter due to all the legal heat. It is unknown why, exactly, Olmstead continued to have any sort of relationship with Hubbard. The prevailing theory is that Hubbard was somehow able to convince the elder bootlegger that he was, indeed, working on Olmstead's behalf and could use his role as an agent to offer protection against any further arrests. For the right price, he could maybe even convince Whitney to drop the matter. Olmstead seemed to accept Hubbard's explanation, and from that point forward, he started paying Hubbard protection money to help keep his operation out of any further legal jeopardy.

For others in the local bootlegging community, Hubbard offered the same type of service: protection against prosecution for the right price. It was a bit of a tightrope act, as Hubbard also had to keep his superiors at the Prohibition office happy. In order to accomplish this, he would randomly pass information along to Whitney and the others about known liquor locations, at which point a raid would be planned. Hubbard would then alert the respective bootlegging operation about the raid, giving them ample time to escape and clear everything out before any federal agents arrived. This kept everyone happy, as he was able to provide the Prohibition office with intelligence about local liquor rackets while local bootleggers felt like their payments to Hubbard were successfully protecting them from arrest. It was a clever scheme that seemed to satisfy both sides, and once again, Hubbard's pockets were flush with cash.

With his financial status once again elevated, Hubbard now had the means to return to his original passion of radio and helped construct

KMO—one of Tacoma's first stations. Soon after, Whitney decided to reassign Hubbard to a nearby logging town. Ever since his outing as an agent, Whitney and others at the Prohibition office could sense that Hubbard's work in Seattle was now compromised. They felt the best course of action would be to give Hubbard a relatively low-level assignment somewhere in a remote region of the state. Not to mention, everyone at the department had reached their wits' end with the eccentric inventor, so having him out of their hair for a few months would be a pleasant break. Hubbard was therefore tasked with uncovering some of the various moonshine stills known to exist throughout Grays Harbor County, particularly in Aberdeen, a flourishing working-class town built

William Whitney. *Author's collection.*

around a thriving logging industry. While Seattle was awash with smuggled Canadian liquor supplied by Olmstead and others, Aberdeen's liquor market was mostly controlled by competing moonshine operations that set up large-scale stills throughout the heavily forested hillsides. Due to its relatively remote location and the fact that it was more than one hundred miles away from the prying eyes of the Seattle Prohibition office, the thirsty region of Aberdeen proved to be one of the nation's hotspots for manufacturing illegal hooch. In fact, next to logging, the second biggest business in Aberdeen was moonshine. Unbeknownst to the Prohibition Bureau, though, Olmstead—wanting to stay out of Whitney's crosshairs—had also recently shifted part of his smuggling operation to the Aberdeen area. It was a lucky coincidence that allowed Olmstead and Hubbard to continue working together.

For Hubbard, the new assignment proved to be particularly enjoyable. His parents resided near Aberdeen, as did a few of his childhood friends, some of whom had become involved in the Grays Harbor liquor trade. This made it easy for him to make the acquaintance of local booze rackets, and he was soon back to his old antics of working both sides for his own financial advantage. It was the same playbook as before—accept payoff money in exchange for protection from arrest.

The new assignment also provided Hubbard and Olmstead with an opportunity to build a radio station in Aberdeen and hopefully resurrect some of the old magic they had previously enjoyed in Seattle. Their biggest hurdle was raising enough money for the expensive construction costs. Hubbard used his charisma to somehow convince Whitney that building a radio station in Grays Harbor would serve as an excellent cover for his secret work as a Prohibition agent. Whitney apparently bought the story, as he not only signed the paperwork for Hubbard to legally incorporate it as a legitimate working radio station, but he even provided some government funds to help Hubbard build it. The remaining costs were covered by Olmstead, who secretly became the station's de facto owner. In fact, the station's call letters were **KXRO**, and unknown to anyone at the time, the "RO" part stood for Roy Olmstead. The station was up and running by early 1927 but only lasted a few months. Local authorities discovered that the station was being used to assist in offshore rumrunning operations and quickly pulled the plug on it. An Aberdeen businessman would later acquire the station from Hubbard in 1928.

Meanwhile, Hubbard had struck up a romantic relationship with Rita, the beautiful woman he had earlier met on the rumrunning ship. At the time, she had been in a relationship with a local smuggler by the name of Winifred

Hubbard sitting on a Seattle court bench in the 1920s. *Public domain.*

"Shorty" Huggett. The recently divorced Hubbard had set his sights on the attractive brunette and was able to charm her away from Huggett. Ironically, Huggett was one of the Aberdeen bootleggers whom Hubbard had been tasked to bring down and whom he eventually delivered to the Prohibition Bureau. Rita and Al fell madly in love during his assignment in Aberdeen and would later get married in Tacoma.

After returning to Seattle, Hubbard resumed his technological pursuits and built radio station KVOS, in the New Washington Hotel, for a man by the name of Louis Kessler. He also returned to his usual set of antics, much to the frustrated dismay of Whitney and others. This time, he would undertake various technological projects but without getting official approval beforehand. In one instance, he showed up at a local Coast Guard base, flashed his badge and told uniformed officers that he was there on "official business" and had been assigned to build radio receivers on their ships so that the Prohibition office could have direct communication with them. Of course, nobody at the Prohibition office knew anything about this until someone from the Coast Guard called in to ask why Hubbard was wanting to board one of their ships to install some suspicious-looking equipment.

Hubbard also set up a radio station in the Prohibition office itself, without anyone's permission, and falsely told administrators there that it had been officially authorized. He then telegraphed Whitney, who was in Washington, D.C., and asked for government call sign letters to be assigned in order to establish communications with the Coast Guard. It was suspected that Hubbard was doing this all on Olmstead's behalf, and both projects were swiftly dismantled. Whitney was quickly losing his patience with Hubbard, though he was naively unaware of the dire consequences that would soon befall everyone involved in Hubbard's double life.

Chapter 3

THE LAST DAYS
OF AGENT HUBBARD

A l Hubbard's final assignment as a Prohibition agent would prove to be his most adventurous. It all started in the spring of 1927, when Prohibition officials were assembling a team of agents to bring down a Canadian rumrunning syndicate that was responsible for smuggling large amounts of whiskey into western Washington. At the time, Hubbard was under heavy scrutiny due to his continued associations with the underworld. Desperate to restore his standing in the agency, he asked to join the team with the explanation that his underworld credentials could provide him with a successful means of infiltrating their operation. In typical Hubbard fashion, he gave a convincing enough spiel that the Bureau hesitatingly granted his request.

With his reputation as an agent now on the line, Hubbard traveled to Vancouver, British Columbia, and paid a visit to the proprietors of this suspected smuggling ring. He knew them from his time with Olmstead and learned that one of their boats had recently been seized by the Coast Guard, causing them to have apprehensions about any future shipments. Hubbard quickly recognized an opportunity in their predicament and proposed that for $1,000, he could use his authority as an agent to help keep the Coast Guard off their backs. At this point, Hubbard's payment-for-protection services were quite well known throughout the bootlegging world, so they agreed to his offer, and a plan was hastily put into place. Hubbard would accompany their next liquor shipment on *Zev*, a sixty-foot speedboat with twin five-hundred-horsepower engines.

The following evening, on May 1, 1927, Hubbard joined the two-man crew of *Zev* as it departed Vancouver. Their destination was Samish Island, a remote finger of land sticking out of the intracoastal region of Washington State's Skagit County, near Anacortes. While not technically an island, its geographical attributes made Samish a popular landing spot for Puget Sound rumrunners. *Zev* had a scheduled rendezvous there with a crew of Seattle bootleggers who would be waiting to purchase their cargo, which included 250 bottles of bonded liquor, as well as a few cases of beer. As the ship left port, the skies grew dark and gusts of wind started churning up the sea. A potent storm appeared to be brewing.

The two men piloting *Zev* were Chris Skrondahl and Laurent Vereecken, veteran rumrunners who were both armed and ready for combat. One of the job hazards of Puget Sound rumrunning was the very real threat of piracy, so most smugglers were prepared to defend their ships if such a scenario presented itself. While chatting with the men, Hubbard noticed that Skrondahl had a large knife strapped to his belt—an important observation given the mission. As the ship piloted through the Strait of Georgia, heavy rain started pouring down and the seas grew increasingly rough. Luckily, *Zev* was built for such conditions and handled the trip well.

When the boat finally reached its Samish Island port, it quickly became apparent that something was amiss. The team of bootleggers waiting for them seemed to be particularly jumpy. As their ship got closer, one of the bootleggers shouted out that they had just been tipped off about an impending raid. As soon as the man spotted Hubbard, his eyes widened and he shouted, "My God! Is that Hubbard? Get that load the hell out of here!" Realizing they had been betrayed, Skrondahl drew his knife, while Vereecken reached for his gun. The storm was tossing *Zev* around pretty good, but Hubbard was somehow able to pull out his revolver and out-draw the two men. A brief struggle ensued, but Hubbard kept his pistol trained on the men, and they eventually raised their hands in surrender. As the *Zev* tumbled about in choppy waters, Hubbard handcuffed the two men to a secure spot on the deck and proceeded to single-handedly pilot *Zev* to nearby Anacortes. It was a wet and grueling trip, but Hubbard's service in Olmstead's rumrunning fleet had prepared him well, and he managed to successfully land the ship and secure it to a dock. Hubbard then marched the two handcuffed men over a mile in the cold rain until he spotted a hotel, from where he telephoned the Coast Guard to send some help. Before long, a team of Prohibition agents arrived, and the two men were placed under arrest and hauled away to jail.

The *Zev*. *Courtesy of Scott Rohrer.*

By all standards, it was a spectacular liquor bust, and Hubbard was widely celebrated for his bravery. Whitney, who was away on business, even called in with a hearty congratulations, adding that his confidence in Hubbard had been restored. The next day, the *Seattle Times* hailed Hubbard's "heroic capture," though in an interview with the paper he downplayed the event, explaining, "It was simply a matter of the rum-runners thinking I was double-crossing the government when I wasn't." Hubbard enjoyed all the subsequent media attention and, for a moment, seemed to have earned himself some actual respect as an agent. Unfortunately for him, the accolades would not be lasting very long.

In the week that followed, Skrondahl and Vereecken—still bitter over being double-crossed—revealed to local newspapers that Hubbard had extorted payoff money from them. Hubbard's corruption as an agent had long been speculated, but this was the first official accusation to confirm such suspicions. This sent major alarm bells going off throughout the federal government, eventually reaching the halls of the U.S. Justice Department. Officials there were dismayed to discover that someone of Hubbard's background had ever been made a Prohibition agent in the first place or that he was still working in an official capacity despite his continued associations with local bootleggers.

In July 1927, two agents from the Bureau were quickly dispatched to launch an official investigation of the matter. They started by looking at Hubbard's finances. Despite his paltry income as a federal agent, Hubbard had purchased a fancy sports car and owned a couple of speed boats, and he and Rita—who sported some eye-catching jewelry—were living in a relatively expensive home. There were other "financial irregularities" as well. For instance, he was paying his ex-wife $169 a month in alimony yet was only earning $150 a month as an agent. Further incriminating evidence continued turning up, and Hubbard was placed on immediate suspension as an agent. Two months later, on September 10, 1927, he was officially terminated from the Bureau of Prohibition. Unfazed, Hubbard simply used his bootlegging connections to continue on in the underworld.

Roy Olmstead's trial was set to begin the following month. Per his original agreement with Whitney, Hubbard was required to be a key witness in exchange for having his name dropped from the grand jury indictments. If he refused to testify, his legal immunity would be taken away and he would be joining Olmstead in prison. As was later revealed, Hubbard also wanted to be reinstated as an agent and knew that a guilty verdict against Olmstead would be a good start toward accomplishing this. It's unclear if he felt morally ambivalent about testifying against his former friend, mentor and boss, though he likely didn't take any great pleasure in it. What is known is that Hubbard took the stand and proceeded to give riveting testimony about Puget Sound bootlegging and how it all operated. He prefaced his presentation by explaining how he had grown tired of "the whole rotten business of bootlegging," which caused him to "volunteer his services as a Federal Prohibition agent." Hubbard then proceeded to describe all of Olmstead's activities in incriminating detail. He explained all the secrets of the illegal liquor industry, as well as the entire process of rumrunning, to a very attentive and fascinated courtroom. After hearing Hubbard's testimony, the jury only took an hour to reach its verdict. Olmstead was found guilty of all charges, with a four-year sentence that was to begin immediately. The King of the Puget Sound Bootleggers was finally headed to prison.

As Hubbard exited the courtroom, the wife of a local bootlegger yelled out at him, calling him a "Judas" and "traitor," and proceeded to hit him with a rolled-up newspaper. Nearby spectators also expressed vocal hostility over his betrayal to Olmstead, and things got so heated that Whitney pulled out his revolver to ward off the aggressive crowd, yelling, "Peace! In the name of the United States!" Hubbard was then escorted to his car by a group of armed guards.

With Olmstead behind bars at McNeill, Hubbard was now a free agent in the bootlegging world and wasted no time in getting back to work. Near the town of Port Townsend, Hubbard and a crew of men were in the middle of unloading 150 cases of liquor when they were surprised by the local sheriff, Phil Chase, and a few of his deputies. Upon seeing the crates of booze, Sheriff Chase ordered his deputies to place all the men under arrest. Thanks to some quick thinking, Hubbard—with the trademark glint of devilish mischief in his eyes—pulled the sheriff aside and produced some of his old federal credentials, falsely explaining that he was a Prohibition agent and that this was all part of an undercover operation. He was convincing enough in his story that the sheriff let the men go along with their entire shipment of booze.

In early 1928, Al and Rita welcomed the birth of their son, William, and moved north to Bellingham, where Hubbard began working as a deputy for the Whatcom County Sheriff's Department. Hubbard made occasional returns to Seattle, including his testimony at the *Zev* conspiracy trial, where Hubbard's corruption as an ex–Prohibition agent was repeatedly brought up by the defense lawyers. In the end, though, the *Zev* crew was found guilty and sentenced to prison.

Hubbard worked as a deputy through the summer of 1928, and at one point, he even invited Whitney and his wife up to Bellingham, where the two families enjoyed a picnic together. By fall, financial difficulties had forced Al and Rita to move back to Seattle. Hubbard was so broke, in fact, that Whitney agreed to loan him some money. As collateral, Hubbard gave him a vial of radium that he had apparently kept from his inventor phase. Hubbard made it a point to stay in regular communication with Whitney, as he desperately wanted to be reinstated as a Prohibition agent. Whitney resisted these efforts and kept telling Hubbard that he should stick to electronics, as that is where his true talents lay. Hubbard was persistent, though, and would visit the Prohibition office once every couple of weeks, occasionally passing various tidbits of information along regarding local bootlegging activity and making every effort he could to ingratiate himself to Whitney. During one of these visits, he made the mistake of attempting to bribe Whitney on behalf of another bootlegger, which proved to be the final straw. Whitney lost his temper and made it abundantly clear that Hubbard was never to return again. The fact that a mysterious "radio telephone" with eavesdropping abilities had just been discovered on the fourth floor of the Prohibition office certainly didn't help matters. Hubbard was now officially persona non grata.

A house in Seattle that Hubbard and Rita lived in. *Author's collection.*

In June 1929, Hubbard paid one final visit to the Prohibition office and, while chatting with some agents, ran into Whitney in the hallway. A heated argument broke out, at which point Hubbard snarled, "Bill, I am damned sick and tired of this fucking government. I have never gotten a square deal, and I am going to beat it with everything I have. They have broken me, and I am going to do everything I can against it. Your Prohibition is no damned good, and from now on I am out to beat it."

Whitney shot back, "Al, you can't come to my office and talk this way about the government, and besides I told you some weeks ago I didn't want to talk to you or have anything more to do with you. I want you to go away and stay away. What you ought to do is go back to your radio business and make a success of it and give up on the idea that you can ever get back on the force."

This would be their last formal interaction, and almost immediately, word started spreading that a vengeful Hubbard had "incriminating evidence" against Lyle and Whitney that was being shared with top government officials. In the fall of that year, Hubbard was confronted on the street about these threats, to which he replied, "I had a good job and Whitney made me lose it. Now I am going after him. It's dog eat dog. You bite me and I bite you, and I am out to get them."

Hubbard made good on his promise and provided closed-door testimony to investigators, resulting in a grand jury indictment against the director of the Seattle Prohibition Bureau, Roy Lyle, and assistant director William Whitney. The ensuing trial became known as the Lyle-Whitney Graft Case. At the heart of the indictment was Hubbard's sworn statement that he collected and distributed protection money at the financial behest of Whitney and acted as an intermediary between liquor rings and Prohibition officials. He also testified how he had turned over the *Zev* payoff money to Whitney. Most of this was dismissed as flimsy testimony, as Hubbard's credibility was considered questionable at best. The trial was excitedly covered by the local press, with one editorial casting doubt on the prosecution by asking, "Have they got the trick words and glib tongue and black heart of Alphy Hubbard?" After nine days, the jury found Lyle and Whitney innocent. Despite the verdict, the damage inflicted on the reputations of the two men was irreversible, especially in the court of public opinion. On May 27, 1930, both Whitney and Lyle were formally dismissed from the Prohibition Bureau. A bitter and angry Whitney returned to his private law practice and, in an ironic twist, was known to have legally represented accused bootleggers.

Hubbard, meanwhile, appeared to have taken Whitney's advice to heart and returned to the radio and electronics world. A group of local aviators had recently incorporated a new airline, Alaska-Washington Airways, and Hubbard was hired to be their radio technician. He spent the next couple of years installing and servicing communications equipment aboard their small fleet of planes. During this stretch of employment, the Hubbard family lived in an apartment building in Seattle's Capitol Hill neighborhood.

It was also during this time that Olmstead was released from prison after serving thirty-four months of his four-year sentence. While behind bars, he underwent a dramatic spiritual transformation and came out a changed person, dedicating the remainder of his life to helping people in need and eschewing any further criminal activity. There is no indication that the two men ever crossed paths again, though when asked by a local newspaper reporter if Hubbard feared retribution, he answered, "It's a possibility. But

Al and Rita at a Seattle courthouse.
Courtesy of Brooke Hart.

they didn't shoot me when I turned in the Olmstead ring, did they? They didn't shoot me when they got out of prison, did they? We've all got to go once. I'm not much afraid."

By March 1932, Alaska-Washington Airways had gone bust, and Hubbard was sent looking for other work. He soon found himself down in California as a temporary employee of the Special Agents Field Division (later to become known as the Bureau of Alcohol, Tobacco and Firearms). He was happy to be working as a government agent once again, especially since his electronics skills were finally being utilized. His first official assignment was to help wiretap the home of San Francisco's top bootlegger, John C. "Johnny" Marino. The results of this wiretapping would be used to help bring indictment charges against Marino, though the records would later be ruled as inadmissible, leading to Marino's acquittal due to lack of evidence. The whole wiretapping affair was somewhat ironic given Hubbard's previous employment with Olmstead. Marino immediately returned to the bootlegging world, and soon after, Hubbard

Hubbard after his California arrest in the 1930s. *Public domain.*

was discharged from the Special Agents Field Division after being accused of extorting money from drivers of suspected liquor vehicles.

After his dismissal, Hubbard borrowed a page from his own playbook and went to work for the very person he had previously been surveilling, working as Johnny Marino's radio technician for the next few years. Marino was running a multimillion-dollar smuggling operation in which large amounts of booze were smuggled from a distillery in Mexico to various Southern California landing spots. This enabled him to avoid paying federal duty taxes on the illicit freight, earning him a considerable amount of money. Just like his glory days in Seattle, Hubbard installed sophisticated communications equipment aboard Marino's speedboats and helped to facilitate all the payoffs that were necessary to keep everything well-oiled and running smoothly. Despite all the precautions, Marino's operation was raided by U.S. Customs agents on March 5, 1936, and Hubbard was among those arrested on smuggling charges. In the hope of a lighter sentence, Hubbard did what was familiar to him in such situations and offered to become a star witness against the other smugglers. Unfortunately, his tactics didn't quite work as planned this time. Despite his testimony, Alfred M. Hubbard was still convicted and sentenced to a two-year prison term. He reported to McNeil Island Penitentiary on September 21, 1936, and would call the prison home for the next couple of years. Some would say it was karmic given this was the same prison where Roy Olmstead had served time thanks to Hubbard's testimony in the Whispering Wires Case. Hubbard would remain as an inmate at McNeil Island until May 21, 1938.

Chapter 4

DAYMAN ISLAND

pon his release from McNeil Island, Hubbard made the decision to remain on the legal side of things and embark on a new path in life. With Rita and William back at his side, he returned to California and was able to obtain a Master of Sea Vessels certification, earning him the lifelong nickname of "Captain." His strong interest in sea vessels was likely a byproduct of his rumrunning days, and he soon became the skipper of a luxury yacht in Santa Monica. During this period, the Hubbards resided in a comfortable home in the sunny suburbs of Huntington Park, and by all accounts, this represented a happy time for the newly reunited family.

While Hubbard was busy chartering boats in Southern California, a chemist by the name of Dr. Albert Hofmann was working on developing a respiratory stimulant at the Sandoz Laboratories in Basel, Switzerland. His research at Sandoz was part of a large-scale program involving the pharmaceutically useful derivatives of plants, and Hofmann's work was focused on ergot, a fungus that grew on rye. From this, he synthesized a new compound that was initially dismissed as not having any medicinal value. It wasn't until 1943 that the true value of the compound—known as lysergic acid diethylamide—would accidentally reveal itself to Hofmann in an extraordinary fashion.

Back in California, Hubbard had assumed command of a charter boat called the SS *Machigonne*. Starting out as a ferry in 1907, the steel-hulled ship was spacious enough that the Hubbards lived aboard it for a year. Meanwhile, things had grown increasingly volatile in Europe following Hitler's rise to power and Germany's subsequent invasion of Poland. France and the United Kingdom had both declared war against Germany, and the growing conflict would soon erupt into World War II. It is here that Alfred M. Hubbard entered another adventurous phase of his life, though the exact details remain somewhat murky.

As Hubbard would later relay the story to friends and acquaintances, he was approached by U.S. intelligence officials in 1941 and asked to participate in a sensitive and covert operation to assist the Allied war effort. This was presumably part of the Lend-Lease Act, enacted in 1941, in which the United States covertly supplied the Allied war effort with food, supplies and weaponry, including ships and planes. At the time, the United States was still considered a neutral country, as it had not yet entered the war, so discretion was of the utmost importance. As the story goes, Hubbard was put in charge of piloting ships to Vancouver, British Columbia, where they were then refitted and sent to England to be used as destroyers in the British navy. To avoid detection, these missions were always conducted at night and without the use of any lights. Hubbard also flew planes to the border, took them apart and towed the pieces to Canada to be sent to the warfront in Europe. A popular legend even holds that Hubbard allegedly was involved in smuggling uranium for use in the Manhattan Project. Presumably, Hubbard's maritime credentials, combined with his intimate knowledge of Puget Sound water routes, made him an ideal candidate for such top-secret operations, with his known talent for electronic communications likely considered an added bonus.

President Roosevelt had reportedly approved of this top-secret operation a full year and a half before the United States entered the war. Some accounts hold that Hubbard was initially approached about joining the operation by the Office of Strategic Services (OSS), a precursor to the Central Intelligence Agency. However, the OSS wasn't formally established until June 13, 1942, which was a year after this top-secret smuggling operation supposedly began and well after America entered the war. Likely, Hubbard would have been approached by U.S. Naval intelligence. In fact, records show that Hubbard's ship, the SS *Machigonne*, was acquired by the U.S. Navy in February 1941, thus supporting the idea that he had been in some form of contact with navy officials when all of this supposedly began.

Hubbard during World War II. *Public domain.*

Hubbard was reportedly involved in these covert operations from 1941 through 1945. As a cover, and to avoid being indicted into questions about political neutrality, Hubbard moved his family to Vancouver, where he became a naturalized Canadian citizen and opened his own business, Marine Sales and Services. For purposes of subterfuge, he was listed as director of engineering for this company. In reality, though, Marine Sales and Services was merely a front for Canada's Department of External Affairs, handling military items sent from the United States and filtering millions of dollars through the American consulate in order to finance the Allied war effort.

Hubbard in the 1930s. *Public domain.*

While Hubbard spent the war serving as America's man in Canada, Albert Hofmann had decided to take a second look at his original ergot compound and began synthesizing a new batch. Toward the end of the process, he began to feel rather strange, and it suddenly occurred to him that he must have accidentally absorbed a small amount of the drug. He decided to call it a day, and after going home, he sat back on the couch and "sank into a not unpleasant intoxicated-like condition, characterized by an extremely stimulated imagination." He was more than intrigued about these strange effects, and three days later, on April 19, 1943, Hofmann returned to his lab and, in the interest of science, decided to intentionally ingest another dose. He estimated that 250 micrograms would do the trick and drank the whole thing down in a diluted glass of water. Nothing happened at first, but within thirty minutes his vision was filled with "an uninterrupted stream of fantastic pictures, extraordinary shapes with intense, kaleidoscope-like play of colors." The experience lasted just over two hours and would be the world's first "trip" of this drug, known thereafter by the compound's acronym, LSD.

A popular version of Hubbard's story maintains that on Christmas Eve 1945, he received an official pardon for his previous bootlegging crimes under Proclamation 2676, in which President Harry S. Truman granted a presidential pardon "to certain persons who have served in the Armed Forces of the United States for at least one year of service." While Hubbard wasn't ever a member of the U.S. military, his continued work for U.S. intelligence reportedly had granted him eligibility. However, later events in the 1960s would call all of this into question.

What is known is that by the war's end, Hubbard's wartime profits had made him into a millionaire. Wishing to continue his scientific pursuits, Hubbard returned to the Pacific Northwest and established the Radium Chemical Company (later the Uranium Corporation) in Vancouver, which was dedicated to the marketing of radioactive elements. He was listed as "A.M. Hubbard, Director of Scientific Research." By all accounts, this was a family affair run by Hubbard, Rita and their son, Bill, who was now nineteen years old—the same age as Hubbard when his atmospheric power generator was first introduced to the world. All the flimflam from his bootlegging days had sharpened his business acumen, resulting in new levels of success and prosperity. He purchased a giant yacht named the *Misinderan*, owned his own small fleet of aircraft and was soon driving around in a Rolls-Royce.

The biggest gesture of his material success took place in 1949. Hubbard decided to purchase his own private island off the coast of Vancouver that would serve as a family retreat for the next twenty years. Dayman Island was heavily forested and surrounded by beaches harboring well-developed oyster beds. To access his new twenty-four-acre sanctuary, Hubbard built a hangar for his aircraft that was made partially from a fallen redwood, as well as a dock for smaller boats and seaplanes. The family lived on one side of the island, and eventually a guest cottage was built on the other side. The home itself was moderately sized with three bedrooms, although it was well furnished and very comfortable. Everything used in the construction had to be barged over from the mainland. Of course, the island included a private space within the hangar where Hubbard could continue his work on various projects and experiments, as well as a large generator within a separate building that powered everything. To get to the island, Hubbard either drove his Rolls-Royce and took the local Black Ball Ferry Line to Vancouver Island, continued on to the town of Chemainus and then hired a water taxi to get to Dayman, or he flew one of his seaplanes.

Perhaps the best description of Dayman Island would be provided nearly a decade later in an exchange of letters between Humphry Osmond and British novelist Aldous Huxley. In one of the letters, dated 1956, Osmond recounts his first visit to Hubbard's island sanctuary:

> *Its shores are honey-colored rock with a few small sandy beaches. It is covered with pine and a juniper like tree. It is sheltered from the blast of most storms. Al's eyrie is a white and blue house on a little headland, with*

Hubbard's Rolls-Royce parked next to
one of his seaplanes on Dayman Island.
Courtesy of Brooke Hart.

*a green lawn in front, and three canoes filled with petunias, snapdragons,
nasturtiums and pansies. All very shipshape as a sailor's home should
be! The island has all the virtues of solitude, seclusion, etc. and none of
the disadvantages of primitive life. It has running water from its own
well, refrigeration, electric lights, hot water. Al has his workshop about
50 yards from the house. It has an air compressor, electric welding, all
sorts of gear, and in the middle his Cessna Seaplane sitting on a carriage.
Next to this, he has his electronics lab full of all sorts of apparatus, x-ray
generators, and all sorts of high-tension apparatus, a psychometer* [a
souped-up lie detector]*, lots of CO2, a radio, telephony equipment.
It is all wholly improbable. In this building he also keeps a power boat
and canoe. So Al is Prospero in his Calinanless island, and every so often
he darts out on his seaplane, over to Vancouver, down to Seattle or to visit
friends on various islands.*

While Hubbard enjoyed his new millionaire lifestyle on Dayman Island,
Hofmann's new drug had created a bit of a stir. His employer, Sandoz
Laboratories, wasn't quite sure what to do with the substance, though it
suspected it might have some psychiatric potential. The company began
providing free samples of the drug to researchers in hopes of finding
profitable applications. In its marketing literature, Sandoz suggested that
psychiatrists take LSD to gain a better subjective understanding of the
schizophrenic experience. And many did.

Meanwhile, despite all his material success, Hubbard had started feeling
an inner restlessness. His lifelong Catholicism combined with his new
island solitude had him asking new philosophical questions that brought
out a certain mystical side. All the electronics and scientific pursuits had
slowly lost their luster as he began looking for something…deeper. He

decided to return to his childhood home in eastern Washington and embark on a spiritual quest, for he knew something bigger was out there waiting for him to find, though he didn't yet know what "it" was. As an acquaintance would later recall of this period, "Al was desperately searching for meaning in his life, but he hadn't the faintest clue what he was supposed to be looking for."

ACT II

To fathom hell or soar angelic
Just take a pinch of psychedelic.
—Humphry Osmond

Chapter 5

TRIPPING THE '50s FANTASTIC

Despite Hubbard's millionaire status, he had inexplicably found himself in the midst of an existential crisis. It was the early 1950s, and up to this point, he had operated under several different titles: inventor, bootlegger, federal agent, prisoner, uranium entrepreneur and spy. Through it all, he had managed to find unbelievable success complete with a luxurious yacht, a two-toned Rolls-Royce and even his own private island estate. Yet something told him that he had still not found his true path. This idea gnawed at him, and for some reason, his thoughts kept returning to his childhood home of Spokane. This eastern Washington town held a special reverence, as he and his siblings had spent countless hours exploring all the nearby forests, rivers and surrounding lakes. He had last visited Spokane in the early 1920s when seeking investors for his first business endeavor, the Hubbard Universal Generator Company, and for some reason, he suddenly felt a strange yearning to return.

Prompted by this strange impulse, Hubbard packed his bags and returned to the Inland Empire for some quiet solitude and self-reflection. The tranquil Spokane woods full of ponderosa pines, Douglas firs and junipers were the perfect setting for this, and Hubbard embarked on several long hikes. During one of these woodland treks, while approaching a clearing, Hubbard reported seeing a familiar golden glow. As he would later tell friends, the same heavenly spirit that had visited him a few decades prior in Seattle suddenly appeared to him again. This time the angel announced that something tremendously important to the future of mankind would be arriving soon in which he would be playing a key role. Upon delivery of the message, the bright glow of the spirit then dissipated into the air and was gone. Hubbard still didn't have any clear answers, but this divine visit assured his mystical side that everything would be settled soon enough, and he returned to Dayman Island, much more at peace with himself than when he left.

Almost a year later, in 1953, Hubbard was reading through a copy of the *Hibbert Journal*—a British quarterly that published scholarly commentary on religion and philosophy—when he stumbled across an article written by Dr. Humphry Osmond about the properties of mescaline, a hallucinogenic derivative of the peyote cactus that had been slowly gaining attention in research and academia. Osmond was a British psychiatrist who served as clinical director of the Saskatchewan Mental Hospital in Canada and was involved in a project studying the use of mescaline in the context of mental health treatment. Starting in the 1940s, an increasing number of intellectuals, artists and writers had been actively seeking out mescaline due to its psychoactive properties, so Hubbard already had a peripheral awareness of the drug. Reading this article further piqued his curiosity. A call was placed, and a meeting was soon set up between the two men at the Vancouver Yacht Club, a swank marina where Hubbard welcomed Osmond aboard his private ship.

As Osmond would later recollect of the meeting, "It was a very dignified place, and I was rather awed by it. Hubbard was a powerfully built man... with a broad face and a firm hand-grip. He was also very genial, an excellent host." Hubbard's eccentric range of interests certainly didn't go unnoticed. "He was interested in all sorts of odd things," Osmond laughingly recalled. Hubbard wished to obtain some mescaline, and as it was still legal, Dr. Osmond supplied him with some. It is unknown where Hubbard's initiation with mescaline took place, though Dayman Island would be the logical guess. From what he later reported, it was a life-changing experience in which he claimed to have witnessed his own conception: "It was the deepest mystical thing I've ever seen. I saw myself as a tiny mite in a big swamp with a spark of intelligence. I saw my mother and father having intercourse. It was all clear."

Interestingly enough, the *Hibbert Journal* article had also captured the attention of noted writer Aldous Huxley. The British intellectual was living in California at the time and wrote Osmond a letter in which he requested a personally guided trip of the drug. With Huxley's well-known literary credentials, Osmond readily agreed and flew to Los Angeles to

Aldous Huxley. *Courtesy of Erowid.org.*

take the famous man of letters on his first mescaline journey. The resulting experience would directly inspire Huxley's next book, *The Doors of Perception*, in which he described his trip as "the most extraordinary and significant experience this side of the Beatific Vision." With Osmond now a common denominator between the two men, Hubbard and Huxley would soon meet and eventually form a lifetime friendship.

In 1954—the same year that *The Doors of Perception* was published—Hubbard himself was actively engaged in the study of mescaline and peyote, which led him to research other known psychoactives. He learned how plant hallucinogens had been used for centuries in various world religions, as well the shamanic practices typically associated with these different compounds. All of this reverberated strongly with his gnostic brand of religion. His pursuit to learn everything he could about psychotropics led him to an article about a revolutionary new drug being manufactured by Sandoz Laboratories. Marketed under the trade name Delysid, LSD was being touted for its various uses and clinical applications in psychoanalysis. As the marketing literature explained, Delysid allowed psychiatrists and mental health researchers the ability to gain valuable insight into what full-blown madness felt like. Most intriguing, though, were the profound transcendental experiences that were being reported while under the influence of LSD. To Hubbard, this new drug sounded very similar to mescaline.

The article was written by British psychiatrist Dr. Ronald Sandison, who had introduced the clinical use of LSD at Powick Hospital in England.

Sandison had pioneered the use of art and music in psychotherapy and, after first hearing about LSD and its possible clinical uses, had traveled to Switzerland, where he personally met Albert Hofmann. He returned to the United Kingdom with one hundred vials of Sandoz LSD and, after discussing the matter with his colleagues, began treating patients with it. From this new form of therapy, Sandison coined the term "psycholytic" (meaning "mind loosening") to describe the drug. He believed this particular property allowed access to areas of the mind not normally accessible.

Hubbard was instantly intrigued by this "mind-loosening" substance and decided to fly to Great Britain to meet Dr. Sandison so he could experience the drug himself. Little is known about their meeting or where, exactly, Hubbard's first LSD experience took place. Most likely, his introduction to the drug happened in a controlled setting at Powick Hospital itself. Dr. Sandison wasn't known to just freely dispense LSD. Rather, per protocol, patients and test subjects would be administered the drug and then left alone in one of the hospital rooms. Typically, these sessions would take place mid-morning, with in-room music provided to those who requested it. A call button was available should a crisis arise, and staff psychiatrists would make occasional rounds to check in and see how things were going. Otherwise, the person was left to navigate the LSD journey entirely on their own. For Hubbard, the resulting experience turned out to be even more jubilantly profound than mescaline. This is what his angel visit had foretold, he realized. This was his true purpose. He became an instant convert, believing LSD to be a powerful utility for opening the human mind. Over the next few years, he would gradually abandon his uranium enterprise while dedicating himself entirely to this powerful new drug and eagerly seeking out others familiar with its use.

In the United States, Boston psychiatrist Max Rinkel had obtained LSD from Sandoz and was the first person to bring it to the country, where he was conducting an LSD study with one hundred volunteers at the Boston Psychopathic Hospital. In New York, psychiatrist Harold Abramson had discovered that small doses of LSD helped facilitate psychotherapy sessions, while on the other side of the country, Hungarian psychiatrist Nicholas Bercel had commenced LSD research in Los Angeles. At the time, the prevailing theory held that LSD produced a "model psychosis." That is, it replicated the same mental state as what a schizophrenic experienced. There was even a word commonly used for this: psychotomimetic, meaning "a mimicker of madness." This attribute quickly caught the attention of some within the U.S. intelligence community who were actively seeking a chemical agent that could be used to break the will of enemy agents and otherwise manipulate human behavior. Rather than utilizing the therapeutic potential of this new drug to help people, these American spooks were more interested in using LSD to control them.

For Hubbard, LSD represented a powerful way to expand the mind, and he now made it his mission to introduce others to its sublime wonders. His life, up to this point, had introduced him to a wide assortment of key and influential people, and these were typically whom he would invite to Dayman Island for the opportunity to experience this new drug, often flying them in on one of his seaplanes. His wife, Rita, was now an active participant in this new mind-expanding pursuit, and the couple would regularly host LSD sessions for their various island visitors. Word traveled fast about the eccentric millionaire from the Pacific Northwest, and Hubbard's name started making the rounds within a growing community of others who were curious about this new mind-illuminating substance. As far as obtaining LSD, Hubbard went straight to the source and purchased forty-three cases of the drug from Sandoz Labs in Switzerland. This was the mid-1950s, and Sandoz—which was hoping to turn the drug into a pharmaceutical success—had no issues with fulfilling such a large order. In fact, when Canadian customs authorities seized the shipment due to Hubbard's papers not being in order, Sandoz quickly intervened to help resolve any administrative hurdles. As a result, Hubbard became the proud owner of a huge supply of pure Sandoz LSD that, over time, would be used to transform the consciousness of hundreds, if not thousands, of people worldwide. This would be only the first of many such purchases that he would be making from the Swiss pharmaceutical company.

It is unknown how many people visited Dayman Island to take part in these early LSD sessions, but the numbers were substantial enough that Hubbard was able to finetune and perfect his techniques within a relatively short period. All the mechanical appliances from his earlier years were now being replaced by the machinery of the mind. He drew inspiration from the shamanic practices of various indigenous cultures, in which initiates were guided through their hallucinogenic trips. Thus, when introducing people to LSD or mescaline, Hubbard saw himself as the captain of a ship taking passengers on a journey of the mind. He was able to recognize that the setting was crucial to the outcome of a trip. A dull and sparsely furnished hospital room, for instance, was not conducive to inspiring a profound epiphany or igniting a round of spiritual ecstasy. And to Captain Hubbard's way of thinking, these transformative effects were where the true

Rita sitting in the Rolls-Royce. The shadow of Hubbard, who was taking the photo, can be seen on the left. *Courtesy of Brooke Hart.*

value of the drug was to be found. While other researchers were clinging to the "model psychosis" viewpoint of LSD, Hubbard was developing ways to harness its consciousness-expanding potential. He built a special room inside his airplane hangar that was dedicated to these LSD sessions. The room was furnished with a comfortable couch and chair, and various works of art—often religious in nature—hung on the walls. Two of his favorites were Gabriel Max's *Jesus Christas* (an optical illusion–style painting featuring the head of Jesus, whose eyes are either open or closed depending on the perspective of the viewer) and Salvador Dali's *Christ of St. John of the Cross*. Music, usually soothing classical, was available. Sometimes, depending how the trip was going, specific songs were chosen to elicit a specific emotional response. If a visitor started exhibiting distress or anxiety, Hubbard would offer reassurance, sometimes pulling out a piece of art to allow the person's focus to be shifted to something both calming and visually beautiful. From all of this, he was able to re-create his own modern version of a shamanic ritual with a promised visit with the Other Side.

Dr. Osmond had remained in contact with Hubbard, sometimes flying out to Dayman Island, and the two men regularly exchanged ideas and new discoveries they were making. Up to this point, Osmond's approach to psychotropic drugs was similar to the "model psychosis" theory. He and a co-worker, Abram Hoffer, had developed the "Hoffer-Osmond Adrenochrome Hypothesis," which posited that schizophrenics overproduce adrenochrome, a byproduct of adrenaline that is structurally similar to mescaline, which then causes the same set of mental symptoms as what a psychedelic trip produces. Hubbard was always dismissive of model psychosis and was known to frequently tell people, "It's easy to make people crazy; what's hard is to make them sane." From his conversations with Hubbard, Osmond gradually incorporated LSD into his research at Saskatchewan, which was now focused on using hallucinogens for the treatment of alcoholism. He all but discarded his previous adrenochrome theory and, with Hubbard's guidance, developed a new form of therapy geared toward helping the patient achieve a peak transcendental experience. In a typical session, the alcoholic patient would be given a single large dose of LSD inside an attractive and well-furnished room (setting was important, reminded Hubbard) and then guided through their journey, with the ultimate goal being the release of repressed psychic material to allow the person to view their condition from a fresh perspective. Dialogue was sparse during the drug experience itself, but a full psychotherapy session was held afterward in which the patient was encouraged to relay any new insights. The results were astonishing, with abstinence rates reaching as high as 60 percent. Best of all, LSD therapy was now viewed as an attractive, cost-effective form of mental health treatment. As a result, Saskatchewan became home to some of the most important such research in the world.

Hubbard's work with Osmond soon caught the attention of Aldous Huxley, who excitedly wrote about this mysterious new figure in a letter to one of his literary associates: "Some new developments might be taking place quite soon in the mescalin field, owing to the appearance of a remarkable personage called Captain Hubbard—a millionaire businessman—physicist, scientific director of the Uranium Corporation, who took mescalin last year, was completely bowled over by it and is now drumming up support among his influential friends." Hubbard's exploits had, no doubt, drummed up a fair deal of excitement, and the letter concluded by adding, "Hubbard is a terrific man of action, and results of his efforts may begin appearing quite soon."

Osmond eventually set up a meeting between Hubbard and his new famous admirer. The two men got along famously but were opposites to an almost humorous degree. Huxley was the epitome of a British intellectual, an articulate and well-read gentleman of the letters, which stood in stark contrast to Hubbard's more rugged and boisterous style of country-boy resolve. While Huxley's genteel approach to life was to analyze it through writing and discourse, Hubbard was prone to simply jump into the middle of where the action was and worry about the details later. The tall, slender Englishman and the stout American renegade represented a genuine odd couple, but they became fast friends and formed a bond that would last a lifetime. After meeting Hubbard for the first time, Huxley wrote this to Osmond:

> *What Babes in the Wood we literary gents and professional men are. The great World occasionally requires your services, is mildly amused by mine; but its full attention and deference are paid to Uranium and Big Business. So what extraordinary luck that this representative of both these Higher Powers should (a) have become so passionately interested in mescaline and (b) be such a very nice man.*

Inevitably, with their friendship now well established, Huxley quickly became interested in a guided LSD session, which the Captain was more than happy to oblige. On Christmas Eve 1955, with a grinning Hubbard at the helm, the British author took his first dose of LSD. The session took place inside Huxley's Los Angeles home, and although he consumed only a tiny amount, the experience was highly significant. He stated:

> *What came through the closed door was the realization—not the knowledge, for this wasn't verbal or abstract—but the direct, total awareness, from the inside, so to say, of Love as the primary and fundamental cosmic fact. These words, of course, have a kind of indecency and must necessarily ring false, seem like twaddle. But the fact remains....I was this fact or perhaps it would be more accurate to say that this fact occupied the place where I had been.*

His previous mescaline journey with Osmond had been unquestionably profound, but he felt that LSD allowed him an even greater understanding of himself, and it inspired the writing of his next book, *Heaven and Hell*.

Having been properly indoctrinated in both mescaline and LSD, Huxley and Osmond now had an important matter to resolve—what to call this category of drugs? The popular term at the time, psychotomimetic, seemed misinformed, if not downright sinister sounding. After all, it wasn't madness they were seeking. In a letter to Osmond, Huxley proposed the word phanerothyme, which means "to make the soul visible." He composed a small ditty to sell his idea:

> *To make this trivial world sublime*
> *Take half a gramme of phanerothyme*

Act II

Osmond responded back with a verse of his own:

To fathom hell or soar angelic
Just take a pinch of psychedelic

Psychedelic! The Greek etymology of the word translates into "mind manifesting," and it seemed to perfectly capture the spirit of these drugs. Osmond presented the term in an academic article, where it immediately took hold and soon became a popular part of the lexicon.

In other circles, LSD was being used for more nefarious purposes. The CIA had officially sanctioned a program known as MK-Ultra, in which various hallucinogens were being actively tested for purposes of mind control and to aid in interrogations. This top-secret government research project had initially tested the effects of such available substances as mescaline, cannabis and opium, but LSD quickly came to dominate many of their experiments, which were becoming increasingly reckless. Unwitting subjects would be dosed with the drug without their consent so CIA agents could secretly observe their reactions. In Operation Midnight Climax, the CIA set up several agency safehouses in San Francisco. These properties were then transformed into makeshift brothels, where government-funded prostitutes would ply unsuspecting johns with LSD-spiked beverages. Agents would then observe everything behind two-way mirrors, often filming the episodes for later study. Such a widespread operation naturally required a steady supply of the drug, and after being turned down by Sandoz, the CIA made arrangements with the Eli Lilly Company in Indianapolis to begin manufacturing large amounts of LSD for use in its operations. With MK-Ultra now in full swing, the CIA actively began recruiting known LSD researchers to help in these covert pursuits.

The psychedelic exploits of ex–OSS agent Alfred M. Hubbard—still fresh in the memories of some intelligence agents due to his covert missions during World War II—had certainly captured the attention of those involved in this top-secret project, and according to Hubbard himself, he was asked to join their team. There is lingering suspicion about the degree of Hubbard's actual involvement in MK-Ultra, especially given his previous employment

Humphry Osmond. *Courtesy of Erowid.org.*

history with the federal government. As Hubbard told the story, though, he didn't approve of what they were doing with his sacramental LSD and declined to be involved in any way. "The CIA work stinks," he would tell friends. "I tried to tell them how to use it, but even when they were killing people you couldn't tell them a goddamned thing.…They're lousy deceivers, sons of the devils themselves."

Later that year, Sandoz sponsored the annual conference for the American Psychiatric Association. Held in Atlantic City, the most discussed topic of the evening was LSD. Dr. Ronald Sandison—the man who had introduced the drug to Hubbard—was the featured keynote speaker and spoke passionately about his work at Powick Hospital. Sandison had never subscribed to the model psychosis theory of psychedelics; rather, he was perhaps the very first person to realize the value in the transcendental properties of LSD, and his pioneering approach to the drug had undoubtedly been highly influential for Hubbard. At the conference, Sandison spoke to a rapt audience about the techniques he employed to help navigate patients through an LSD session and the amazing results he was seeing from this. Aldous Huxley was among those confirmed to be in attendance that night. It is unknown if Hubbard joined him or not, though it seems unlikely that Hubbard would pass up a chance to visit with his unofficial mentor or to hobnob with others in this exciting new field.

The mind-expanding properties of LSD led Hubbard to become quite well versed in human psychology, particularly in the growing field of psychoanalysis. In fact, while working on developing his own brand of psychedelic therapy, Hubbard even corresponded with Carl Jung, in which he asked the famous psychoanalyst to offer his views on the psychological benefits of hallucinogens. In a letter addressed to "A.M. Hubbard," Dr. Jung replied back with a polite but terse criticism of any such benefits:

> *When it comes to the practical and more or less general application of mescalin, I have certain doubts and hesitations.…Mescalin is a short cut and therefore yields as a result only a perhaps awe-inspiring aesthetic impression, which remains an isolated, unintegrated experience contributing very little to the development of human personality. I have seen some peyotees in New Mexico and they did not compare favourably with the ordinary Pueblo Indians. They gave me the impression of drug addicts.*

He concluded his letter, "Hoping you are not offended by the frankness of my critical opinion, I remain, dear Sir, Yours very truly, C.G. Jung."

Despite such a sharp rebuke from the founder of analytical psychology, Hubbard continued full throttle as a psychedelic buccaneer. He was always on the go, zipping from one destination to another on his worldwide mission. On any given day, he could be conferring with Dr. Osmond in Saskatchewan; visiting Huxley in Los Angeles; meeting with LSD researchers in Europe; or instructing curious mental health practitioners in New York City on the proper techniques for a guided LSD trip. It was from Hubbard that several key psychiatrists in Southern California were able to obtain LSD while also being instructed on the importance of "set and setting." The late Oscar Janiger, a noted psychotherapist who ran a popular practice in Hollywood, was one such recipient of Hubbard's LSD sermons and gleefully reminisced about the Captain's visits, where he would freely share samples from his Sandoz goody bag. "We waited for him like the little old lady on the prairie waiting for a copy of the Sears Roebuck catalogue," he chuckled.

Meanwhile, as Hubbard crisscrossed the globe, he began hearing murmurs about a group of engineers and computer scientists in San Francisco who were expressing a strong interest in experiencing one of his guided trips. They were located in a stretch of land that would eventually become known as Silicon Valley, and being a fellow inventor and technician himself, the good Captain had every intention of paying them a visit.

Chapter 6

THE TAIL OF THE UNIVERSE

With his reputation firmly established, more and more people began seeking out Hubbard's psychedelic services. He claimed to be in possession of the world's largest stockpile of LSD, which nobody ever questioned given his seemingly endless supply. By this time, other drugs had also been added to his pharmacopoeia, and he traveled with a leather briefcase full of pure-grade LSD, mescaline and psilocybin (a hallucinogenic compound found in certain species of mushrooms that had also been synthesized by Albert Hofmann and was now being manufactured by Sandoz). Back in the 1920s, when out promoting his atmospheric power generator and explaining its mysterious mechanics, Hubbard had proclaimed that he had "hitched his wires to the tail of the universe." That had been over three decades ago, and he was now on a worldwide mission as a traveling LSD apostle. His earlier laboratory full of tubes, electronics and various arcane instruments had since been replaced with an attaché case full of hallucinogens responsible for expanding the minds of the era's greatest thinkers. And while he no longer pursued engineering, his wires were still quite fully hitched to the universe's cosmic tail.

By the mid-1950s, Hubbard had also discovered the unique properties of a gaseous compound known as carbogen—a 70 percent oxygen, 30 percent carbon dioxide mixture that came in a small, portable tank and was known to have a peculiar entheogenic effect. Known as Meduna's Mixture (after its inventor, Ladislas Meduna), carbogen was popular among early

LSD researchers for its use as a hallucinogenic litmus test: patients would breathe in a few lungfuls of the gas through a mask, and depending on their reaction, it would then be determined if they were a good candidate for LSD therapy or not. Those who reacted negatively to carbogen would typically be vetted out, while all others would usually be approved for the final round. Carbogen was known to induce a state of abreaction that allowed people the ability to explore the unconscious contents of their minds and then purge unwanted and repressed emotional material. Because of this, carbogen soon became a regular part of psychedelic therapy, as its cathartic effect allowed for a smoother LSD experience and decreased the risk of there being any existential turbulence along the way.

Hubbard became quite fond of carbogen. He always had a tank or two on hand, and it soon became a regular part of his repertoire. LSD initiates would first be given several large lungfuls of Meduna's Mixture to "clear away the problems," and then it was on to the main course. The late Betty Grover Eisner, PhD, a noted American psychologist, would later write about her LSD and carbogen experiences with Hubbard:

Al was the grand old man of LSD, of consciousness change…large, rambling, and with his own private plane and special island on Puget Sound. He had tanks of oxygen and carbon dioxide. This was the first time I had experienced or seen the Meduna technique of inhaling "carbogen" for altered states of consciousness in order to help deal with psychological problems. I was to find that 6 to 10 inhalations, or "sniffs" helped as preparation for my LSD session and then was useful in working to dissolve problems which arose afterwards. This was a remarkable technique which patients hated more than any other but also knew how effective it was in helping solve psychological problems. I applaud it for the remarkable work it accomplished.

Hubbard also fancied Meduna's Mixture for his own personal use. Visitors to Dayman Island often reported that Hubbard kept scuba tanks of carbogen in his boathouse and kept ducking out to take hits from the tanks. Aldous Huxley's wife even recounted a memorable day when they invited Hubbard to their house:

He showed up for lunch one afternoon, and he brought with him a portable tank filled with a gas of some kind. He offered some to us, but we said we didn't care for any, so he put it down and we all had lunch.

Act II

He went into the bathroom with the tank after lunch and breathed into it for about ten seconds. It must have been very concentrated, because he came out revitalized and very jubilant, talking about a vision he had seen of the Virgin Mary.

Meanwhile, in Palo Alto, California, an informal group of intellectuals, religious leaders and pacifists was holding regular meetings to discuss such matters as spirituality, world peace and matters of the mind. These meetings would eventually become known as the Sequoia Seminars. During one of these conferences, a philosopher named Gerald Heard gave a lecture to the group about his personal experiences with the consciousness-expanding powers of a new group of drugs known as psychedelics. Listening to Heard's presentation that night was Myron Stolaroff, a high-ranking engineer at an early tech company known as Ampex. A growing industry of similar such companies was starting to emerge in a valley south of San Francisco, and Stolaroff oversaw long-range planning at his electronics firm. Stolaroff had been inspired to become involved in the world of technology when, as a student at Stanford University, he witnessed the demonstration of the first commercial oscillator by David Packard and Bill Hewlett, who would later form the Hewlett-Packard Company. After the end of World War II, Stolaroff earned an engineering degree and, in one of his first jobs, would help develop a prototype for the first magnetic reel-to-reel recorder, directly leading to the formation of Ampex. Despite his success in the tech world, Stolaroff felt there was no spiritual center to his life and so found himself drawn to the deep philosophical ideas that were being explored at the Sequoia Seminars. Upon hearing Heard's presentation about the transformative effects of these new drugs, he instantly became curious and started corresponding back and forth with Heard. In one of these letter exchanges, Heard described an LSD experience he had involving a strange man from the Pacific Northwest named Al Hubbard, who was becoming known as a kind of wandering shaman—flying from city to city with his briefcase full of mind-altering drugs. A few days later, in a weird moment of synchronicity, Stolaroff was having a group discussion at work when the chairman of the board at Ampex began telling everyone about this "fabulous character in Canada" he had recently met who was changing people's lives with a new class of mind-expanding drugs. He was, of course, speaking about Hubbard. After hearing about this mysterious figure from two different people, Stolaroff wasted no time in writing Hubbard a letter expressing his spiritual concerns and asking for more information on LSD.

A month later, in February 1956, Stolaroff looked up from his desk at Ampex to suddenly see Hubbard standing in the doorway with a sly smile on his face and a tank full of carbogen. Al apparently still enjoyed paying surprise visits to people's offices, just as he did back in his days as a Prohibition agent. Stolaroff's first and immediate impression of Hubbard was as a person who "radiated an enormous energy field." After their formal round of introductions were properly handled, the Captain wasted no time in setting Stolaroff up for the first step of psychedelic therapy by having him take several lungfuls of carbogen right there in his office. The two men launched into a deep philosophical conversation, and an immediate friendship was formed. Stolaroff would later claim that Hubbard left a deeper impression on him than anyone he had ever met before and wrote this about their initial encounter:

> *What a contrast between he and me! Here I was, slight of build, deadly serious, extremely introverted, trembling at whether others approved of me or not, anxious to follow all the rules and conventions of society. And here was he, large in body, constantly grinning, with a mischievous twinkle in his eye, turning everything into fun. He was voracious in his appetites for all that life had to offer, and a great belittler of all that ordinary persons held dear. What a combination—my staid character that didn't wish to tread on anyone's toes, and he, constantly looking how to upset the status quo and produce some excitement.*

The first day of their meeting, Hubbard took Stolaroff to a nearby motel where he and Rita were staying. Stolaroff was given more carbogen, which he described as giving him a "glimpse, and especially a feeling, of another world. The contact was magical. Never before had I felt such euphoria." Al and Rita had another destination they needed to depart to, but the two men remained in contact, with Stolaroff continually pressing Hubbard for an LSD session. Hubbard wanted to wait until spring so he could fly Stolaroff up to Dayman Island and have the experience ideally take place on their picturesque island estate when everything was in bloom. But Stolaroff was too impatient, and so an earlier session was planned. At the time, the Hubbards were renting an apartment in Vancouver for use during their stays on the mainland, and it was decided that this would serve as the location for Stolaroff's first LSD session. With Al and Rita as his guides, Stolaroff took several deep breaths of carbogen, followed by sixty-six micrograms of Sandoz LSD. During the next several hours, he reportedly relived the trauma

Myron Stolaroff. *Courtesy of Erowid.org.*

of his own birth, which made him realize that many of his own psychological issues could directly be traced back to his initial entrance into the world. It was an important epiphany for him that would have taken years of psychoanalysis to attain, and yet he reached this conclusion in only one LSD session. It was quite the transcendental rush, and Stolaroff returned to Ampex convinced that LSD was the greatest discovery that man had ever made.

Upon his return to California, Stolaroff made it his mission to turn others on to the wonders of this new drug and started holding weekly sessions for some of the more adventurous staff at Ampex. Engineers from such nearby tech firms as Hewlett-Packard, Burroughs and General Electric also became involved. Stolaroff convinced this small group that LSD could expand their level of technological creativity and make their jobs easier. This was the dawn of the computer age, which was partially being shaped by a new wave of humanism seeking to use technology to enhance—not replace—the human mind. LSD was a perfect fit for this mind-expanding mission of theirs, and from this group of electrical engineers came many of the technological innovations that ultimately paved the way for the development of the personal computer. A few members of this psychedelic crew would later be involved in the creation of ARPAnet, the precursor to the world wide web. It was a creatively fertile time for these technological visionaries, and their innovative work would eventually pave the way for such start-ups as Adobe, Cisco and Apple. To their way of thinking, the sky was the limit, and hallucinogens helped make impossible ideas into reality. Hubbard became a regular fixture at these Silicon Valley LSD sessions and actively helped Stolaroff in his attempt to transform Ampex into a psychedelic-based corporation.

Not everyone was enamored of all these changes, however. Ampex still had a substantial number of the more traditional, buttoned-down workers who had no interest in having a "mystical" LSD experience. This included many of Ampex's top executives, who were dismayed to see how Stolaroff's LSD sessions were starting to change the focus of the company. One day, Hubbard came down from Canada to take Stolaroff and his intrepid group on a weeklong LSD retreat up in the Sierra Mountains. Hubbard's influence on Stolaroff had created simmering tensions at Ampex for some time, and now this eccentric mystic was taking some of the company's top workers out to a remote cabin for an entire week so they could all take a drug that, incidentally, still had a reputation for inducing a state of madness. For many in the firm, this was the final straw. An emergency meeting was held in which one of the top executives stood up, pounded his fists on the table and angrily demanded to know, "What if this nutball drives our best men crazy?!?"

When the men returned a week later, nobody seemed to have lost their sanity, but the lines in the sand had been clearly drawn, and Stolaroff found himself being slowly ostracized within the company. His association with Hubbard was no longer appreciated. A few years later, to the relief of many at the firm, he would finally resign from Ampex and found his own venture. By this time, however, the seeds of psychedelics had been firmly planted in early tech culture. Stolaroff always gave Hubbard full credit for this and would remark, "I was convinced that he was the man to bring LSD to planet Earth."

In addition to Silicon Valley, Hubbard was still working with Dr. Osmond and Dr. Hoffer in Saskatchewan, Canada, as well as with several psychiatrists throughout the United States. His unique brand of psychedelic therapy had earned a well-respected reputation for its effectiveness, and his services were in high demand. It probably didn't hurt that he was still the largest North American supplier of pure Sandoz LSD. These activities inevitably caught the attention of certain officials within the medical establishment who loudly began questioning Hubbard's credentials and whether he should be allowed to administer such powerful psychotropic drugs when he wasn't a licensed physician. For many people, this would spell the end of the road. For Hubbard, who had spent nearly his entire life developing ways to bypass the official system, the whole brouhaha was merely an inconvenient bump in the road. He simply enrolled in a correspondence course at Taylor University—a less-than-esteemed academic outlet being run out of Colorado Springs, Colorado. Many dismissed the institution as being nothing more than a diploma mill, but by the end of the year, Hubbard had procured a PhD in biopsychology. He was now Dr. Alfred M. Hubbard, clinical therapist.

Throughout all this, Hubbard remained a devout Catholic and still regularly attended mass at the Cathedral of the Holy Rosary, a beautiful Gothic Revival church in the heart of Vancouver. He had befriended a priest there, and in 1957, this holy man agreed to participate in one of Hubbard's personally guided LSD sessions. By all accounts, it was a spiritually profound experience for the parishioner that he enthusiastically recommended to others in his congregation. In a letter dated December 8, 1957, the newly enlightened Reverend J.E. Brown announced on official church stationery that he had been introduced to LSD and championed the drug by proclaiming that "true intellectual knowledge is the honorable objective of man's inquisitive intellectual faculties." He concluded his letter with a written prayer: "We humbly ask Our Heavenly Mother the Virgin Mary, help of all who call upon Her, to aid us to know and understand the true qualities of these psychedelics, the full capacities of man's noblest faculties, and according to God's laws, to use them for the benefit of mankind here and in eternity."

A little over ten miles east of the cathedral, in the British Columbia municipality known as New Westminster, sat a beautiful turn-of-the-century mansion. In 1919, a physician by the name of Dr. E.A. Campbell purchased the estate and transformed it into a fifty-five-bed medical facility. Named Hollywood Hospital, after the grove of holly trees that surrounded the property, the cedar and stone manor became known as a place for alcoholics to detox and kick the habit. In 1956, Dr. Campbell died in an accidental drowning accident, and the hospital was then taken over by Dr. J. Ross MacLean, a suave and high-profile psychiatrist who continued the hospital's mission as an alcoholic treatment facility. It didn't take long for MacLean to make the acquaintances of Hubbard, who by this time had perfected his own mind-expanding ways of treating alcoholism. MacLean was taken in by Hubbard's charm, confidence and growing reputation and saw the potential for enormous financial success in Hubbard's unique form of therapy. The two men agreed to become business partners of sorts, with Hubbard being given control of an entire wing of the hospital. It certainly didn't hurt that, by this time, Hubbard had become Canada's sole licensed importer of Sandoz LSD. In no time at all, the two men worked diligently together to transform Hollywood Hospital into one of the world's top locations for psychedelic therapy. At first, they focused on the hospital's original mission of treating alcoholism, but over time, they included other psychological disorders as well. During their time together, MacLean and Hubbard would supervise more than three thousand acid trips.

With a PhD now sitting next to his name, as well as the new title of "director of research," Dr. Hubbard wasted no time in transforming his wing of Hollywood Hospital into an impressive LSD facility. Always a big

The Cathedral of the Holy Rosary in Vancouver, British Columbia. *Courtesy of Todd Brendan Fahey.*

Cathedral of the Holy Rosary
646 Richards Street
Vancouver 2, B.C.

INTRODUCTION TO LSD EXPERIENCE

Friends:

    True scientific knowledge is the honourable
objective of man's inquisitive intellectual faculties.

    The sciences have divided into myriad sections
the vast, seemingly limitless data that is ours to learn.
Over the centuries man has gained collectively drawing on
his predecessors and sharing with his colleagues and suc-
cessors.

    Each division of scientific knowledge has pro-
duced proof conclusive of the Supreme Being responsible
for the perfection of order our scientific minds uncover.

    We are aware of man's fallibility and will be pro-
tected in our studies by that understanding and recognition
of the First Cause of all created things and the laws that
govern them.

    We therefore approach the study of these psychodelics
and their influence in the mind of man anxious to discover
whatever attributes they possess, respectfully evaluating
their proper place in the Divine Economy.

    We humbly ask Our Heavenly Mother the Virgin Mary,
help of all who call upon Her to aid us to know and understand the true qualities of these psychodelics, the full
capacities of man's noblest faculties and according to God's
laws to use them for the benefit of mankind here and in
eternity.

Dec 8/57   Rev J. Brown

Letter from the Cathedral of the Holy Rosary, written by the Reverend J.E. Brown, after his introduction to LSD by Al Hubbard. *Courtesy of Erowid.org.*

proponent of the importance of setting, Hubbard furnished each room with a comfortable couch and throw pillows. Pleasant artwork adorned the walls, and hi-fi stereos would play the music of Bach, Beethoven and Mozart. He even had an entire private suite built for him with a fireplace and giant sofa. His therapy sessions were much the same as what he developed on Dayman Island. He would first have the patient sample carbogen to see if they were a suitable fit for LSD therapy. If so, he would then have them write out their autobiographies, recounting their trauma and hang-ups. After their psychological profiles had been determined, Hubbard would then bring them a crystal chalice filled with liquid LSD, and the guided session would officially begin. A single high dose of LSD (usually three hundred to four hundred micrograms) was the standard at

Hollywood Hospital. With Hubbard as your guide, years of psychoanalysis could be packed into a single day.

Word soon spread about this Canadian hospital, which was now boasting recovery rates of up to 90 percent, and in no time at all, the rich and famous started arriving by the droves to receive help in overcoming their battles with the bottle or to receive some form of psychological care. The roster of celebrity patients included Robert Kennedy's wife, Ethel Kennedy; crooner Andy Williams; and actress Mimsy Farmer. Several Canadian politicians were also rumored to have paid a visit. "This was an elite, private facility where people could pay to get a safe space to experience a psychedelic," writes author and scholar Erika Dyck, PhD. "There was a lot of glitz and glamour and it's shrouded in these really fantastic rumors."

In 1957, the *Province*—a Vancouver newspaper—assigned one of its reporters, Ben Metcalfe, to investigate a story about the whereabouts of Canadian Forestry minister Robert Sommers, who had suddenly gone missing from his official duties. It didn't take Metcalf very long to follow the trail of clues, leading him directly to Hollywood Hospital, where he learned that the politician had been staying. He started looking into this mansion-turned-hospital, and preliminary research told him that he had stumbled on an even bigger story than anyone had possibly imagined. Speaking to locals, the reporter learned that the hospital had managed to maintain a certain level of secretiveness, though some rather sensational rumors were starting to surface. "Mystery hung over it like a cloak," wrote Metcalfe. The newspaperman was eventually able to set up an interview with MacLean, though once inside the hospital he quickly realized that the real star of the show was an unusual character whom everyone referred to as Dr. Hubbard. Metcalfe observed how the two men seemed to work well together but keenly described the harmonious dichotomy between them: "MacLean was tall, handsome, well dressed—a smooth mixture of business and medicine. Hubbard was a squat, slightly rumpled, wryly jocular and supremely confident gnostic." The resulting exposé proved to be a hit series for the newspaper, generating a lot of media attention and helping to catapult Metcalfe's career as a successful journalist.

Two years later, in 1959, Metcalfe returned to the hospital, this time wanting the LSD experience for himself. With Hubbard as his personal steward, Metcalfe ingested four hundred micrograms of LSD and took a twelve-hour guided trip, leading to yet another series of fascinating articles for the *Province* in which he described his trip as being "thrust into the blast furnace of truth." At one point, the profundity of his session elicited a

The LSD room at Hollywood Hospital. *Courtesy of Todd Brendan Fahey.*

visceral reaction, and Metcalfe started weeping uncontrollably. "This is all repressed masculinity," Hubbard said, consoling him. "This is what we bury to become men." It was a pivotal experience for the young journalist, who would later channel his passion for the environment by founding the activist organization Greenpeace. Besides taking LSD himself for the assignment, Metcalfe was also able to sit in and observe a guided session and was granted interviews with some of the hospital's patients. One woman he talked to had quit heroin after a long addiction, and several others had successfully kicked their alcoholism. According to Metcalfe, the treatment was "the most dramatic experience made accessible to the human mind."

With such high-profile patients now coming through the doors, especially amid all the good press generated from Metcalfe's articles, MacLean began charging as much as $1,000 per LSD session, a rather extravagant fee at the time and quite unaffordable to anyone except the wealthiest. This set off a philosophical dispute between the two men, as Hubbard held firm to his views of LSD being a spiritual and therapeutic tool rather than a moneymaker. It was quite the departure for Hubbard, who back in the Prohibition days had brazenly offered his services to the highest bidder. Psychedelics had seemed to temper his impulses as a confidence man, and the disagreement between the two men spilled out into the open as Hubbard loudly protested MacLean's commodification of these sacred drugs. Eventually, Hubbard left the hospital over the dispute. He had several other irons in the proverbial fire and certainly didn't need the hospital to fulfill his vision. MacLean, meanwhile, would continue offering high-priced LSD sessions at the hospital, becoming a very wealthy man in the process. In 1975, after most psychedelics had become criminalized, MacLean sold the property to developers and used the proceeds to purchase one of Vancouver's most lavish residences, known as Casa Mia. Somewhat ironically, the mansion was once owned by George Reifel—Vancouver's top bootlegger during the Prohibition era and a one-time associate of Hubbard's. As for the hospital itself, it was demolished and replaced by a shopping complex known as Westminster Mall. All the files from the hospital were suspiciously procured by a one-time employee and are now privately held in the B.C. Archives, leading to further intrigue surrounding the legendary facility. As of the writing of this book, a documentary about Hollywood Hospital is reportedly in the works.

By the late 1950s, LSD had swept through California, especially in areas where Hubbard had previously focused his efforts, including Los Angeles and San Francisco. The Hollywood psychiatric community, where Hubbard first planted his psychedelic seeds several years earlier, had by now firmly embraced LSD therapy, and a new movement had blossomed. The California psychiatrists to whom Hubbard had initially introduced LSD had, in turn, introduced the drug to other psychotherapists who, in turn, introduced it to others, and on it went in an endless psychedelic domino effect. Sandoz Laboratories, which was celebrating the financial success of LSD's growing popularity, was more than happy to sell large quantities of the drug to any mental health practitioner who needed it for "research." One of these psychiatrists, Mortimer Hartman, acquired his own stash of Sandoz LSD and opened the Psychiatric Institute of Beverly Hills. Over the next few years, many famous celebrities would seek out Hartman's services, including Cary Grant, who underwent over one hundred LSD sessions at the famous institute. "After weeks of treatment came a day when I saw the light," Grant reported in a published interview with *Look Magazine* in 1959. "When I broke through, I felt an immeasurably beneficial cleansing of so many needless fears and guilt. I lost all the tension that I'd been crippling myself with." Grant's enthusiasm for the drug helped popularize its treatment, and Tinseltown was soon awash in psychedelic therapy being offered to the rich and famous. Many of these

Gerald Heard, Aldous Huxley and Al Hubbard in the 1950s. *Courtesy of Erowid.org.*

Hollywood psychiatrists followed the same template that had originally been developed by Hubbard, complete with carbogen followed by a single high dose of LSD taken inside a handsomely decorated therapy room. The roster of celebrity patients who sought these services would include such luminaries as Stanley Kubrick, Jack Nicholson, Anais Nin and James Coburn. Naturally, this caught the attention of some of the era's top publications, which began writing glowing reports about the promise of LSD and its growing use in psychiatry. This included *Time* magazine, which published several different reports on the attributes of psychedelic therapy, praising LSD as "an invaluable weapon to psychiatrists."

As the 1950s came to a close, Hubbard was reputed to have introduced more than six thousand people to LSD. "Most people are walking in their sleep," Hubbard said in an interview. "Turn them around, start them in the opposite direction and they wouldn't even know the difference. But give them a good dose of LSD and let them see themselves for what they are." His pioneering work was starting to receive credit in various academic publications, including *The Handbook of the Therapeutic Use of LSD-25*, a highly influential work published in 1959 that acknowledged

Hubbard's influence in its opening pages: "It will be obvious to the careful reader but it is a pleasure to acknowledge here as well, the debt which the authors owe to the work of Dr. A.M. Hubbard."

As Hubbard and his colleagues welcomed the dawn of a new decade, they could sense that the culture of psychedelics was beginning to change. Throughout the 1950s, the traffic in LSD belonged to a middle-aged set of tweed-clad intellectuals, psychiatrists, researchers and early computer engineers. However, a new dawn was approaching, and psychedelics would soon be popping up on the streets of such places as San Francisco, Seattle, London and New York. A much more youthful and rebellious counterculture would soon embrace the

Hubbard during his time at Hollywood Hospital. *Courtesy of Todd Brendan Fahey.*

drug, displacing the older guardians of LSD and recreationally using the drug to "turn on, tune in and drop out." Indeed, the 1960s would be a tumultuous decade in which everything changed, and as always, Hubbard would find himself right in the middle of everything.

Chapter 7
WHEN THE GENIE ESCAPES

The beauty of the natural world always held a special allure for Hubbard, and by the dawn of the 1960s, the Mojave Desert had become one of his favorite destinations. Aldous Huxley had previously purchased a remote cabin there, which he used as a writing retreat, and this is likely how Hubbard was first introduced to the desert location. He found himself particularly entranced by the barren scenery of Death Valley; the colorful rock formations and scattered Joshua trees amid the desolate landscape provided an idyllic setting, and with a head full of Sandoz LSD, the sunsets there were particularly stunning. These desert sojourns were always a majestic experience for Hubbard and any others who would often accompany him. During one such trip, with the sun setting in the distance, Hubbard and Stolaroff found themselves entangled in a deep conversation fueled by whatever hallucinogen they happened to be on. From this discussion arose an epiphany that they should establish their own psychedelic research center. Things had grown extremely strained at Ampex, and Stolaroff was more than ready to explore new career options.

With an energetic and confident Hubbard at his side, Myron Stolaroff resigned from Ampex in 1961 and established the International Foundation for Advanced Study (IFAS) in Menlo Park, California. Other scientists and engineers from a variety of backgrounds also joined the foundation, whose mission was the use of psychedelics to explore human potential and creativity. Willis Harman—a professor of engineering at nearby Stanford University— was brought onboard to serve as vice president. Because of Stolaroff's prominent role, the foundation's clientele was largely composed of people from the nearby tech community, thus cementing the symbiotic relationship between early LSD research and the emerging computer industry. In fact, one of the foundation's regular clients was a man by the name of Doug Engelbart, whose later claim to fame was the invention of the computer mouse. The foundation quickly gained a reputation as one of the top leaders for psychedelic research and published its findings in a variety of scientific journals, including the *International Journal of Neuropsychiatry*. The influential essay "The Psychedelic Experience: A New Concept in Psychotherapy" would become a seminal work in the respective research field.

While Stolaroff served as director of the foundation, Hubbard was its true mastermind. With his status as the largest individual supplier of Sandoz LSD for the American market, he made sure that the foundation's hallucinogenic stockpile was always kept full. Additionally, the rooms at IFAS were all of Hubbard's design and his therapeutic methodologies were used exclusively. Guided sessions at the foundation always included an initial interview, followed by carbogen testing. As Stolaroff explained, "In our Foundation work with clients, we found that several treatments with Meduna's mixture was an excellent procedure to introduce novices to altered states of consciousness. Many discovered unconscious contents of their mind for the first time. The procedure also cleared away a good deal of repressed material, thus freeing the subject for a smoother, more profound psychedelic experience." After the carbogen, a single large dose of LSD would then be administered, followed by a psychotherapy session afterward to analyze the results. The foundation charged $500 for each therapy session, and it soon became one of the top destinations for those looking to expand their minds.

While IFAS celebrated its successful launch, Al and Rita maintained their Pacific Northwest retreat on Dayman Island. Various celebrities and movie stars were known to fly in for secret psychedelic rendezvouses with the Hubbards. It was a happy time for the couple despite the loss of Hubbard's parents. First, his mother passed away in Tacoma, Washington, in 1960, followed by the death of his father in Los Angeles in 1961. Despite the losses, Hubbard continued onward on his mission and even began experimenting with other psychedelics. This included his first encounter with dimethyltryptamine (DMT), in which Hubbard was injected with the drug by a known psychiatrist, who then recorded the session on a tape recorder. In the recording, Hubbard reported having an incredible sense of gratitude as well as "feeling a big wonderful responsibility regarding being able to use these materials. There is nothing to be afraid of. Its hitting power

Myron Stolaroff, Jean Stolaroff, Al Hubbard and Willis Harman during the 1950s. *Courtesy of Erowid.org.*

is like carbogen." He also described the visuals: "The designs resemble Aztec designs…beautiful fish but without any flesh on them…a fish skeleton. Beautiful streams of color, very friendly. A pull sideways in time towards the back…as if a wind were blowing." Afterward, he concluded that "D.M.T. would be very valuable in psychiatry."

Hubbard dreamed of setting up a series of clinics in order to train other LSD researchers. He procured a gram of LSD (roughly ten thousand doses) from Sandoz, which he kept in a safe-deposit box in the duty-free section of Zurich's airport. From there, he was able to ship quantities of the drug without paying a tariff. The Swiss government eventually caught up with him, and he was promptly deported. Undeterred, he simply found other ways to obtain Sandoz LSD from outside Switzerland's borders.

The popularity of Stolaroff's foundation inspired other such research centers, and before long, Palo Alto and Menlo Park—the municipalities that form California's Silicon Valley—became hotbeds of psychedelic research. This included some rather secretive experiments being conducted by Stanford scientists at the Menlo Park Veterans Hospital, which, unbeknownst to the outside world, was being coordinated by the CIA as part of its MK-Ultra

Project. One of the volunteer test subjects for this project was a young writer named Ken Kesey, who enrolled in the Menlo Park drug trials as a way to earn some money. For seventy-five dollars a session, Kesey eagerly ingested whichever hallucinogenic drug was given to him while government-backed scientists dutifully recorded his physiological responses. Kesey found the mind-expanding properties of these drugs to be quite enjoyable, particularly one that the researchers kept referring to as LSD. He wanted to explore these substances on his own, though, and soon accepted a job at the hospital as the nighttime janitor. With everyone gone for the evening, he would set aside his mop and bucket and sneak into the medical supply room in order to pilfer some LSD for his own personal consumption. His observations at the Menlo Park Hospital, as well as his drug experiences, would subsequently inspire the writing of his famous novel *One Flew Over the Cuckoo's Nest*. During the writing of the book, Kesey introduced LSD to his friends, and they were soon regularly holding group drug sessions. Eventually calling themselves the Merry Pranksters, Kesey's crew began holding regular acid parties in the San Francisco area, not too far from Stolaroff's foundation, that rapidly gained in popularity. This new and younger group of psychedelic aficionados had no interest in guided sessions inside a stuffy research room. Their approach was much more bacchanalian, where the psychedelic landscape was freely explored in a festive group setting, and any previous therapeutic model was eschewed in favor of simple, hedonistic fun. By 1964, Ken Kesey and the Merry Pranksters would paint a school bus in festive dayglo colors and drive it across the country in order to spread the gospel of acid and poke fun at the world of squares. LSD had broken free from the controlled environments of the universities, laboratories and research centers where it previously resided and was now slowly seeping out into the general populace. The psychedelic genie had officially escaped its bottle.

Over on the East Coast, a similar movement was starting to blossom. Two psychology professors at Harvard University had found themselves embroiled in controversy following some ethically questionable experiments involving the use of psilocybin. One of the professors, a respected PhD by the name of Timothy Leary, had been introduced to hallucinogenic mushrooms during a trip to Mexico in 1960. The experience convinced him that such a substance had unlimited possibilities in the psychological field, and he returned to Harvard dedicated to studying and researching its use. Joining him in this academic endeavor was another hallucinogenic-friendly professor, Richard Alpert. With university grant money, Leary and Alpert placed an order for a very generous amount of pharmaceutically pure psilocybin from Sandoz

Laboratories, and over the next two years, the two men carried out a series of experiments known as the Harvard Psilocybin Project. In the beginning, these experiments were conducted in strict accordance with all academic guidelines. The project quickly gained the respect of Stolaroff and others, who hoped that Leary's studies would lend some academic legitimacy to their profession.

Naturally, such an ambitious project soon caught Hubbard's attention, and the elder statesman of psychedelics decided to pay the younger professor a visit. As Leary would later recall of the encounter:

> *He blew in laying down the most incredible atmosphere of mystery and flamboyance, and really impressive bullshit! He was pissed off. His Rolls Royce had broken down on the freeway, so he went to a pay phone and called the company in London. That's what kind of guy he was. He started name-dropping like you wouldn't believe…claimed he was friends with the Pope.*

When asked if he believed all of Hubbard's claims, Leary unhesitatingly and matter-of-factly replied, "Well, yeah, no question!" Hubbard showed Leary his bag full of LSD, which he wanted to swap for some of Leary's psilocybin, and the two men agreed on a mutual exchange of one Sandoz-manufactured hallucinogen for another. Hubbard also pulled a tank of carbogen from his car and allowed the Harvard professor to have a few breaths. "The thing that impressed me," Leary recalled, "is on one hand he looked like a carpetbagger con man, and on the other he had these most-impressive people in the world on his lap, basically backing him."

After Hubbard's visit, Leary and Alpert gradually incorporated LSD into their experiments, which were slowly becoming blurry in terms of what academic value was actually being achieved. Word spread around campus that Leary and Alpert were taking psychedelics along with the students, causing widespread concern among the Harvard faculty. When reports surfaced that undergraduate students had become involved and were taking these drugs without any medical supervision—

Timothy Leary. *Courtesy of Erowid.org.*

something that was strictly against the rules of such academic research—the whole project started to look less like a legitimate study and more like a drug-fueled party. Concerned about the direction that this research had taken, formal complaints were filed, and in May 1963, Timothy Leary and Richard Alpert were both summarily dismissed from their teaching positions at Harvard University.

Fortunately for Leary, his psychedelic exploits had caught the admiration of some very wealthy benefactors, who invited the ex-professor to come live at their sixty-four-room mansion in New York, known as the Millbrook Estate. Leary established the sprawling mansion as the headquarters for his own unique brand of psychedelic research. He also began making some rather controversial statements in which he promoted the recreational use of these drugs. At the same time, LSD started appearing on the streets in sugar cube form, making it relatively accessible to the young, curious and inexperienced. From all this, unfavorable stories started appearing in magazines and newspapers warning parents about the potential dangers of this new drug. This sudden flurry of bad press raised immediate concerns among the psychedelic research community, many of whom had worked hard to legitimize LSD's therapeutic benefits. They were starting to grow frustrated over Leary's antics and would later place the blame for all this negative publicity at his feet. "I liked Tim when we first met," commented Hubbard. "He seemed like a well-intentioned person but then he went overboard....I warned him a dozen times."

LSD's negative media coverage attracted renewed political scrutiny, resulting in new drug safety regulations quickly being enacted by the U.S. government. Its days as an easily available research drug were quickly ending. Previously, any entity that claimed to be conducting research had as much legal access to Sandoz LSD as was needed. In response to American political pressure, though, Sandoz enacted a more stringent set of protocols regarding its distribution of LSD. By 1963, a committee of investigators would now review the scientific legitimacy for each and every request of the drug and advise Sandoz if the respective research project met the required criteria. If a researcher did not pass these new investigative hurdles, then no LSD would be given. Many psychedelic research centers now found themselves without any access to Sandoz LSD, including the International Foundation for Advanced Study. Sandoz concluded that neither Hubbard nor Stolaroff possessed the necessary medical credentials now needed for access to the company's psychotropic offerings, and the foundation was pharmaceutically cut off at the knees. Undeterred, Hubbard simply boarded a plane and, with his trademark glint of mischief, flew off to Europe in search of a new supplier. As it turned out, a Czechoslovakian chemical corporation known as Chemapol had recently started manufacturing pure-grade LSD, so Hubbard paid them a visit and worked his charm. Not only did he obtain a large supply of LSD on behalf of the foundation, but he also negotiated a business agreement where he was now Chemapol's representative for the entire North American research market.

After securing this new source of LSD, Hubbard returned to Canada and set up his own psychiatric clinic in downtown Vancouver. As with his other arrangements, Hubbard partnered with an actual psychiatrist and placed himself on the payroll as a "consultant." By all accounts, the Consera Psychiatric Clinic was a small and off-the-radar type of operation that never enjoyed the fame or popularity of Hollywood Hospital or IFAS, and perhaps that was Hubbard's intention.

November 22, 1963, will forever live in infamy as the date of President John F. Kennedy's assassination in Dallas, Texas. The tragic event was covered by media outlets worldwide and was front-page news for the next several months. Overshadowed by such a major news story on that day was the passing of another important figure. Aldous Huxley had been battling laryngeal cancer for several months, and his final hours were spent at home with his wife, Laura, at his bedside. Unable to speak and knowing that death was at his door, Huxley feebly scribbled a note to Laura: "LSD, 100 µg, intramuscular." She obliged, and Huxley bid farewell to this mortal coil while peacefully floating in the psychedelic realm. He was sixty-nine years old.

After his passing, Laura Huxley wrote a letter to Al and Rita, detailing his last moments. A few months later, Dr. Humphry Osmond, Myron Stolaroff, Willis Harman and Hubbard decided to take LSD together as a memorial to Huxley's life. Thanks to Stolaroff, the subsequent discussion was captured on a reel-to-reel recorder, providing some interesting insights into the state of affairs for psychedelic research at that time. Based on their recorded discussion, this original crew of men seemed to have some degree of awareness that their world was being taken over by a new generation. Timothy Leary, in particular, was singled out and criticized by the group for using LSD to "start a new religion." At some point during the conversation, Osmond metaphorically referred to Hubbard as a "killer," which prompted Al to recall his days as a Prohibition agent:

> *During my several years work as an agent of the government, I had many occasions—not a few occasions, but MANY occasions—where if I had*

Hubbard mowing his yard in California. *Courtesy of Todd Brendan Fahey.*

wished to harm anyone, I had all the excuse necessary to do so. I think I should say I have never harmed anyone. I have shot over people's heads, close enough to them—even through their clothes—but I have never harmed anyone. Nor have I had the desire to do so. But should the need arise [pause] *the capabilities are there.*

By the mid-'60s, Hubbard had developed a personality conflict with the foundation's medical doctor, prompting him to submit his resignation from his time at IFAS. Hubbard left the organization owing Myron Stolaroff nearly $100,000. After several months of no communication between the two men, an angry Stolaroff eventually realized that Hubbard had no intention of repaying what he owed, prompting him to remark, "He was a sonofabitch: God and the Devil, both there in full force.…He was an expert in discerning one's weaknesses and playing upon them to his advantage." Despite the unpaid debt, Stolaroff never forgot Hubbard's influence: "Hubbard made a deeper impression on me than anyone I had ever met. It was an impression that radically altered my whole value-belief system, and completely changed the course of my life." At some point, the two men resumed some degree of correspondence and were eventually able to rebuild their friendship.

Magazine articles were increasingly warning about the dangers of LSD, and its growing popularity as a recreational drug was starting to cause widespread concern. With political pressure steadily mounting, the federal government enacted a series of legislation known as the Drug Abuse Control Amendments, which were designed to criminalize its use. In response, Sandoz made the decision to stop the production and distribution of LSD altogether. In a public statement, released in August 1965, Sandoz explained, "In spite of all our precautions, cases of LSD abuse have occurred...completely beyond the control of Sandoz. We can no longer bear the responsibility for the allocation and distribution of these substances." Several months later, Sandoz would also stop the production of psilocybin. This prompted the beginning of underground LSD laboratories, and street acid was soon widely available on the black market.

With the future of psychedelic research now in serious jeopardy, Hubbard began entertaining other ways to earn a salary and soon accepted a job at Teledyne in Beverly Hills, California. Teledyne had originally established itself as a major technology firm and was now a major subcontractor for the Department of Defense. The exact details of Hubbard's employment at Teledyne remain somewhat shrouded in mystery. Some accounts say he worked as a "human factors analyst," testing the effects of psychochemical agents on military personnel in order to "develop techniques in areas of military interests." Other sources maintain that Hubbard's employment at Teledyne involved a secret NASA project in which astronauts and pilots were given psychotropic drugs. This has certainly given rise to speculation regarding Hubbard's possible involvement with MK-Ultra. There is also a more innocuous account of Hubbard's time at Teledyne that maintains that he simply worked as a "procedures analyst" for a research project involving the physiological effects of aviation in order to assist pilots with the physical stressors of flight. Given Hubbard's area of expertise, the first scenario seems much more plausible than the second, though the truth of the matter will likely never be known.

The spring of 1966 saw the passing of another important figure from Hubbard's past when Roy Olmstead died at the age of seventy-nine. Hubbard's relationship with Olmstead had been complicated, and there is no indication that the two men ever spoke again after Olmstead's trial in the late 1920s. Interestingly, both of their post-prison storylines share a similar redemptive arc. During Olmstead's incarceration, he discovered the Christian Science religion, and following his release, he dedicated himself to salvation for his earlier crimes. The remainder of his life was spent working a series of low-paying jobs while living a very meager existence, and much of his free time was spent volunteering to help rehabilitate ex-prisoners. Whenever asked about his previous life as Seattle's King of the Bootleggers, he would simply reply, "That Roy Olmstead doesn't exist anymore." Likewise, Hubbard had been a lifelong Catholic whose spirituality received a high-voltage charge with his discovery of LSD. He had also abandoned his criminal past, with much of his post-prison life spent developing the fundamentals of psychedelic therapy in the interest of helping others. Both men had dedicated themselves to enacting positive social change, and like Olmstead, Hubbard would also soon find himself living a more meager existence. As Olmstead neared the end of his life, his exciting backstory as Puget Sound's top bootlegger had been mostly forgotten, and few people even remembered who he was. Olmstead died in a tiny Capitol Hill apartment, and his obituary was buried toward the back of most Seattle-area newspapers.

A few months after Olmstead's death, Hubbard's one-year contract with Teledyne expired, and except for some sporadic work as a freelance psychiatric consultant, he found himself unemployed. Al and Rita still owned Dayman Island, though their primary residence was now an apartment in Hawthorne, California. Psychedelic research centers were quickly disappearing thanks to all the new regulatory measures, as was Hubbard's primary means of earning a living. His psychedelic exploits had evaporated most of his savings, and he realized that he now needed a steady job. He applied for a variety of positions in the technology field but found that his status as an ex-con was seriously interfering with his success at landing a job. As a result, he applied for a presidential pardon with the Department of Justice in order to have his criminal record expunged. This prompted the FBI to conduct a background check on him to evaluate his post-prison conduct. All his associates wrote exemplary character affidavits for him, and Hubbard was personally interviewed at the FBI office in Inglewood, California. Hubbard reported that he was still able to earn a small income as a "psychiatric drug consultant" (presumably for his clinic in Vancouver) but that his previous 1936 bootlegging conviction "had caused him considerable embarrassment in seeking employment." Ultimately, Hubbard's request for

Al and Rita standing in a courtyard, circa 1960s. *Courtesy of Brooke Hart.*

a pardon was denied. An official reason was not provided, though the likely culprit was Hubbard's direct and long-standing association with LSD. By this time, the federal government had developed a very unfavorable view of the drug, and this is likely what sealed Hubbard's fate.

Public panic about LSD was further exacerbated by a 1966 *Life* magazine article titled "LSD: The Exploding Threat of the Mind Drug that Got Out of Control." The article acknowledged the drug's original usefulness in psychotherapy, but much of the content concerned all the "bad trips" resulting from its growing popularity on college campuses. It referred to the current psychedelic scene as a "cult," and Timothy Leary—who was then being held in jail on marijuana charges—was named as the ringleader. Stories started circulating about college kids jumping from rooftops after LSD made them think they could fly or going blind after staring at the sun for several hours. A popular urban legend at the time told the horrifying tale of a married couple arriving home after an evening out only to discover the babysitter high on LSD and that, in her intoxicated state, she had mistaken their newborn baby for a pot roast and had baked it alive in the oven. Calls for a nationwide ban soon followed, and the government, at both state and federal levels, began forming committees and holding public hearings regarding the social dangers of LSD. In the U.S. Senate, politicians heard from a variety of experts on both sides of the equation. A few doctors testified that LSD causes psychosis and "the loss of all cultural values." On the other side of the aisle, others argued that, if used properly, LSD had tremendous therapeutic value. Senator Robert Kennedy (whose wife, Ethel, had benefited from LSD therapy) defended the drug against all the rampant hysteria, stating, "Perhaps to some extent we have lost sight of the fact that it can be very, very helpful in our society if used properly." In the end, Kennedy's words fell on deaf ears, as the FDA only added further restrictions, thus furthering LSD's demise as a psychiatric tool.

That same year, the California state senate formed a fact-finding committee in order to examine the potential dangers of LSD. Hubbard testified as an expert witness at one of these senate panels in which he carefully explained LSD's importance and usefulness as a psychiatric tool, including its success in treating alcoholism. Humphry Osmond, meanwhile, wrote to various American officials, pleading with them to help protect medical research. Unfortunately, their efforts fell flat, as California signed a bill into law on October 6, 1966, which made it illegal to manufacture, sell or possess the drug. This was the coup de grâce for any last remnants of psychedelic research in California. Hubbard still had an impressive

Hubbard in the 1960s. *Courtesy of Todd Brendan Fahey.*

supply of pharmaceutically pure LSD and immediately moved his stash up to Canada, where it was still legal. For a brief time, he and Stolaroff considered reestablishing the IFAS in Vancouver.

By 1967, the countercultural movement was in full swing, with San Francisco serving as the unofficial epicenter. By now, Kesey's LSD parties had grown into the "Acid Tests," attracting hundreds of people to downtown warehouses where revelers drank freely from giant LSD-laced punch bowls and danced to the music of popular house band the Grateful Dead. Hippies from all over the country started arriving in droves to take part in the festivities. This massive psychedelic immigration to the Haight-Ashbury district of San Francisco became known as the Summer of Love.

Watching from the sidelines, Hubbard and his associates were less than thrilled over the freakshow spectacle of the whole thing. To their way of thinking, Kesey and Leary had been reckless and irresponsible in their handling of LSD, resulting in the sudden demise of psychedelic therapy. All their hard work and accomplishments were now gone thanks to the horde of long-haired kids hanging out in Golden Gate Park. Hubbard, in particular, was enraged over what had happened to his sacred LSD. This brought out the more law-and-order, conservative side of Hubbard. As one of his associates would recall, "Al was really an arch-conservative, he really didn't like what the hippies were doing with LSD, and he held Timothy Leary in great contempt." Hubbard maintained that LSD should only be administered and monitored by trained professionals, though this revealed a certain level of hypocrisy, as Hubbard and his cohorts had been regularly enjoying psychedelics in a recreational, non-therapeutic manner for over a decade. In fact, they were the first group to have done so. Nevertheless, Hubbard was quickly growing impatient with the antics of the American left. In response, he shaved his hair to a buzzcut and started wearing a military-style outfit, complete with holstered pistol at his side. Captain Hubbard was back, and his new appearance recalled his days as a Prohibition agent. He even started hobnobbing with the political right; he and Rita attended the inaugural ball for Republican governor Ronald Reagan, where the two men discussed the illegal drug trade. There were even rumors that Hubbard had assisted the San Francisco district of the

Drug Enforcement Agency (DEA) to help bring down black market LSD laboratories, which were increasingly popping up on the streets. A new era of Prohibition had emerged—this time for psychedelic drugs—and once again, Hubbard found himself as a "shadowy figure who worked both sides of the street."

Meanwhile, Leary continued to strip away any aura of respectability or scientific legitimacy that LSD once had when he began urging his followers to "tune in, turn on and drop out." For this, Hubbard harbored a simmering level of anger and resentment. Dr. Humphry Osmond would later recall a time that he became very alarmed after the two men had taken some psilocybin together and Hubbard started expressing his homicidal thoughts out loud. "Al got greatly preoccupied with the idea that he ought to shoot Timothy," Osmond remembered, "and when I began to reason with him that this would be a very bad idea I became much concerned that he might shoot me." Luckily for Leary, such impulses were stifled when Hubbard was offered a new job from one of his previous work associates.

Willis Harman was a Seattle native who had graduated from the University of Washington in the 1940s with a degree in electrical engineering. Afterward, Harman accepted a position at Stanford University, where he taught engineering and physics. After his first LSD experience in the late 1950s, Harman developed an interest in humanistic psychology and taught a popular graduate seminar called "The Human Potential," which covered topics ranging from meditation to psychedelic drugs. It was during this time that he made the acquaintance of Stolaroff and Hubbard, leading to his involvement with IFAS. After the foundation was disbanded, Harman resumed his work at Stanford, where he was appointed director of the Stanford Research Institute (SRI), a scientific research organization involved in several different projects. Harman was assigned to work on the Alternative Futures Project, which, as the name implied, performed future-oriented strategic planning for corporations and government agencies. With all the social and political unrest happening at the time, the secretive project was tasked with investigating the nearby countercultural movement taking place in Haight-Ashbury. Given Hubbard's recent transformation into a staunch law-and-order defender of "the old days," as well as his previous experience as a Prohibition agent, Harman knew Al would be a good fit for this project. In October 1968, Harman invited Hubbard to join SRI as a "special investigative agent." As Harman would later admit, though, "Al never did anything resembling security work." In his written job offer to the Captain, he wrote:

ACT II

Our investigations of some of the current social movements affecting education indicate that the drug usage prevalent among student members of the New Left is not entirely undesigned. Some of it appears to be present as a deliberate weapon aimed at political change. We are concerned with assessing the significance of this as it impacts on matters of long-range educational policy. In this connection it would be advantageous to have you considered in the capacity of a special investigative agent who might have access to relevant data which is not ordinarily available.

Hubbard, who had been desperate for a steady paycheck, promptly accepted the offer and would serve as a security officer for SRI through the mid-1970s. "His services to us," explained Harman, "consisted in gathering various sorts of data regarding student unrest, drug abuse, drug use at schools and universities, causes and nature of radical activities, and similar matters, some of a classified nature." The crew-cut Hubbard, attired in his khaki paramilitary uniform, had grown extremely disdainful toward the long-haired hippies who, to his way of thinking, were abusing his sacred psychedelics and demonizing them in the public eye. Thus, he took these new job duties extremely seriously, applying his espionage talents toward infiltrating this new countercultural menace.

Some would say that these undercover efforts at SRI exposed several intellectual dishonesties regarding the use of psychedelics, therefore inviting a series of questions. Namely, why was it acceptable for the rich and famous to enjoy the benefits of psychedelics at research centers but not the college kids hanging out at Haight-Ashbury? Should LSD only be available to those who could afford to pay for a guided session? Were guided therapy sessions the only appropriate way that hallucinogenic drugs should be experienced? Hubbard and Harman seemed to have abandoned their former proletariat views of psychedelics and were now devoted to the idea that LSD should only be administered by trained professionals and that street use was dangerous. Adopting the trickle-down theory of conservative economics, Hubbard even had plans to introduce the drug to the top echelon of business and political leaders. According to Dr. Abram Hoffer, "Al had a grandiose idea that if he could give the psychedelic experience to the major executives of the Fortune 500 companies, he would change the whole of society."

Despite Hubbard's undercover role in helping to infiltrate the hippie movement, his own psychedelic activities were not immune to new drug laws that were becoming increasingly enforced. In a sudden and sweeping move, the FDA—which Hubbard had previously assisted—ordered its agents to seize all remaining psychedelics not accounted for by Sandoz. Psychiatric offices and any remaining research centers were abruptly raided, and anything associated with LSD research was immediately confiscated. Hubbard begged Abram Hoffer and Humphry Osmond to allow him to hide his stash of LSD at their Canadian psychiatric facility, but they didn't want to attract any unwanted attention and hesitatingly refused his request. Out of desperation, and to avoid possible prosecution, it was reported that Hubbard buried his remaining inventory of LSD somewhere in Death Valley, where it presumably remains to this day—a psychedelic treasure chest waiting to be discovered. When governmental panic finally subsided, only a small handful of scientists could continue LSD research, and none of them was connected with Hubbard or any of his associates.

Hubbard continued his surveillance work at SRI, but his finances were dealt a lethal blow when the doors of any remaining research centers were officially closed for good. As a result, Hubbard was forced to sell his beloved island sanctuary. The sale of Dayman Island would serve as a symbolic end to Hubbard's days in the psychedelic realm. According to reports, Hubbard piloted a ship to his former Pacific Northwest retreat; loaded it with antiquated electronics, old laboratory equipment and expensive furniture; and left Dayman Island for California, never to return again.

Chapter 8

THE DEATH AND LEGACY
OF CAPTAIN TRIPS

A s the '60s drew to a close, LSD had firmly established itself as the era's hallmark drug just as psychedelic therapy was taking its last dying breath. The irony of the situation certainly wasn't lost on Hubbard and his colleagues. Sandoz LSD had been replaced with street acid, the most popular of which was a variant known as Orange Sunshine. The San Francisco area had been almost entirely taken over by the peace-and-love hippie crowd with their drugs, antiwar activism and "good vibes," though other, more dangerous elements were also beginning to settle in. In the summer of 1969, a small group of LSD-fueled destitutes—led by a charismatic ex-con named Charles Manson—would carry out a horrific string of murders in the Los Angeles area, thus casting a dark shadow over the so-called Age of Aquarius. Over on the East Coast, mere days after the Manson killings, the Woodstock Rock Festival was attended by almost a half million people. During the large musical gathering, a young up-and-coming artist named Jimi Hendrix wowed the audience with his guitar version of "The Star-Spangled Banner" that he famously played while under the influence of LSD. By 1970—despite the dark stories being reported from Southern California—an estimated two million Americans had used the drug.

The popularity of such a powerful substance certainly wasn't lost on the American government. In 1970, the U.S. Congress passed the Controlled Substances Act, which put all federally regulated substances into one of five schedules based on such criteria as medicinal value, harmfulness and potential for abuse or addiction. Under this new act, signed into law by President

Richard M. Nixon, LSD was placed in Schedule 1, which is reserved for what are believed to be the most dangerous drugs with the highest potential for abuse. Simple possession of LSD was now deemed a felony punishable by up to fifteen years in prison. This new classification also restricted LSD research to nonhuman subjects unless a special approval was granted by the FDA. Just prior to passage of this law, Hubbard utilized his powerful connections and reportedly spoke personally to Vice President Hubert Humphrey, who then took the cause of LSD into the Senate chamber, with unsuccessful results. Once a promising form of therapy, LSD had now been officially criminalized in the United States.

Other countries soon followed. In 1971, LSD was made illegal throughout most of Europe, and a few years later, the National Institute of Mental Health determined there to be no medical benefits associated with LSD and immediately halted all related research projects. Meanwhile, the popularity of psychedelics continued to skyrocket. Blotter acid (LSD-impregnated sheets of paper printed with colorful art) emerged on the streets as the most popular form of the drug. Timothy Leary—now a fugitive of justice from some earlier marijuana-related arrests—was proclaimed to be "the most dangerous man in America" by President Nixon.

By this time, Hubbard was still working at SRI but had officially retired from any LSD activity due to all the stringent new drug laws. Despite his retirement, his earlier introduction of the drug to 1950s-era Silicon Valley was starting to bear the psychedelic fruits of his early labors. Several of the technology firms that Hubbard had been involved with, including Stolaroff and the International Foundation for Advanced Research, had evolved and splintered off into new companies—many of which were now devoted to computer science. One such tech aficionado had developed a fondness for LSD while in college and, from those early psychedelic experiences, had begun entertaining creative ways to make computers more accessible to the general public. He would eventually join a small crew of other like-minded engineers in Palo Alto, California, where they toiled in a garage on a groundbreaking project that would soon revolutionize the computer industry. His name, of course, was Steve Jobs. Their project, known as Apple 1, was named after an apple farm where Jobs had previously enjoyed several LSD trips. He would later describe LSD's influence on his pioneering work on personal computers:

> *Taking LSD was a profound experience, one of the most important things in my life. LSD shows you that there's another side to the coin, and you*

can't remember it when it wears off, but you know it. It reinforced my sense of what was important—creating great things instead of making money, putting things back into the stream of history and of human consciousness as much as I could.

Up near Hubbard's old stomping grounds in Seattle, another computer engineer by the name of Bill Gates was known to have dabbled in LSD. It has often been speculated that without psychedelics, the personal computer might have never been invented.

In 1974, Hubbard's contract with SRI ended, and he went into semi-retirement, splitting his time between Vancouver and Menlo Park, California. The Canadian government had adopted similar laws regarding LSD, and all the country's psychedelic research centers were subsequently put out of business. In 1975, after British Columbia pulled all government funding from Hollywood Hospital, Hubbard's old business partner Dr. MacLean sold the property to developers for a tidy sum of money and retired a very wealthy man. The old building was torn down and replaced by the Westminster Mall, which still occupies the space today. During his trips to Vancouver, Hubbard would often stop in Seattle, perhaps to revisit some of the people and locations from his earlier years. It was a new world, and very few people—including those in the psychedelic community—knew who Hubbard was or were aware of his contributions. By this time, his son, Bill Hubbard, had established himself as an engineering consultant in the chemical industry down in Los Angeles.

Hubbard in his later years.
Courtesy of Todd Brendan Fahey.

By the late 1970s, Hubbard had developed heart disease and was reportedly in and out of various hospitals. He and Rita had a small manufactured home built in Casa Grande, Arizona, where they lived out their remaining years. It was a humble home but was filled with all the belongings from their earlier, more luxurious years, making it a cozy retreat. Hubbard had become much more reclusive and was never far from a tank of home oxygen that he used to help him breathe. In 1978, he made one last effort to legitimize psychedelic therapy when he petitioned the FDA to authorize the use of LSD for terminal cancer patients. Perhaps this was inspired by Aldous Huxley's

Al and Rita at the beach. *Courtesy of Brooke Hart.*

famous pre-mortem use of the drug, or maybe Hubbard's own mortality was starting to weigh on his mind. Either way, it was a humanitarian gesture, as research showed that a properly guided psychedelic session provided peace of mind and a much greater acceptance of death for those with terminal illness. Hubbard applied for an Investigational New Drug (IND) application and furnished the FDA with two decades' worth of clinical documentation from his earlier years. Before the FDA would even entertain such a request, however, there were several research hurdles that needed to be completed. It was an enormous task, and Hubbard attempted to recruit assistance from some of his former colleagues. In the end, nobody had much enthusiasm for such a formidable assignment, as psychedelic research had been effectively snuffed out almost a decade earlier. Without the strength to carry on alone, Hubbard soon abandoned the project. "He knew that his work was done," remembered Willis Harman.

The last public glimpse of Hubbard occurred in 1979, at the Los Angeles home of Timothy Leary, who hosted an "acid reunion" for all the psychedelic pioneers from the early days. The whole soirée was videotaped and featured most of the original crew, including Dr. Humphry Osmond, Oscar Janiger, Myron Stolaroff and Laura Huxley. Al and Rita were both present, and apparently, any former animosity between Hubbard and Leary had been tempered, as the fuzzy film clip shows the two men sitting cordially right next to each other for the entire event. Hubbard was still sporting a military buzz cut and was attired in his "Captain Hubbard" uniform with an unknown patch on the sleeve of his right arm and a badge pinned to the left breast pocket. Throughout the gathering, everyone takes turns reminiscing about the good old days, with the conversation offering an interesting portal into the original first wave of psychedelic research. This would be the last known sighting of Hubbard.

Alfred M. Hubbard finally succumbed to heart disease and exited the world for good on August 21, 1982. In his eight decades of life, he was a fascinating figure who occupied several different titles that were often paradoxical in nature: criminal and cop; psychedelic pioneer and anti-hippie crusader; scientist and shaman; government agent and renegade; hustler and humanitarian. Indeed, this dual nature defined much of his life. He was "god and the devil, both in there full force," his friend and associate Stolaroff once observed. Hubbard passed away peacefully at his Arizona home with Rita at his side. He was eighty-one years old. It is unknown if the original Captain Trips was on any hallucinogens when he left this mortal plane.

Al Hubbard and Humphry Osmond reminiscing over old times at Timothy Leary's house in 1979. *Courtesy of Todd Brendan Fahey.*

Hubbard's death generated little publicity as, by that time, his story had mostly faded into obscurity. It wouldn't be until nearly two decades later that his earlier work would start regaining recognition when a new generation of scientists resurrected the fundamentals of psychedelic research that Hubbard and his cohorts had originally developed. Beginning in the late 1990s, the psychology world saw a renewed interest in the therapeutic potential of hallucinogenic drugs, and there are currently a number of clinical trials underway to test the potential benefits of such substances as psilocybin, ketamine, MDMA and even LSD to treat such disorders as depression, PTSD and addiction. Thanks to these renewed efforts, there are signs that the government is willing to loosen up previous restrictions on such research. Recently, the FDA approved a clinical trial for testing the use of MDMA to treat veterans with PTSD, and similar trials are also underway involving the use of psilocybin for depression. There is still plenty of bureaucratic red tape blocking the way of such research, but there is also a growing optimism that things are moving in a positive direction.

With all these new research efforts, Hubbard is finally starting to receive due credit for developing many of the templates for this visionary form of therapy. He was not only one of the first people to see LSD's function as a visionary or transcendental drug, but he was also able to realize its therapeutic potential. From this, he developed many of the fundamentals for such therapy, including the importance of "set and setting"—that is, the state of mind and the surrounding environment in which a drug experience takes place. From Dayman Island, he used these principles to construct one of the first rooms dedicated to psychedelic therapy with such staples as comfortable furnishings, music and pleasant, often mystical-themed artwork. He also encouraged the use of a single large dose of LSD to guarantee a transcendental experience, pre-augmented with a few breaths of carbogen, followed up by a psychotherapy session to assist the patient in analyzing the results. At this point, it is unknown how many of these elements will be adopted by those currently involved in psychedelic therapy's renaissance, though Hubbard's influence looms large and his pioneering work in this field is beginning to attract more and more attention.

Throughout the computer industry at large, Hubbard's influence also casts a wide shadow. He served as an early prototype for what would become the unconventional Seattle tech genius, laying the groundwork for such personalities as Bill Gates, Paul Allen and Jeff Bezos. In Silicon Valley, he became the "Johnny Appleseed of LSD," planting the seeds that are still widely felt today. In fact, "micro-dosing" has emerged as one of the hottest trends among the IT crowd. In this practice, tiny, sub-perceptual doses of LSD are taken daily to help fuel creativity. The amount taken isn't enough to feel any psychedelic effects but reportedly allows for a much sharper and more creative focus. A recent online piece about micro-dosing reported that that practice was rampant throughout Silicon Valley.

Hubbard's overall influence was probably best captured in a letter that the father of LSD, Albert Hofmann, wrote to Steve Jobs in 2007. Hofmann had just celebrated his 101st birthday and, despite his advanced age, was clearly excited about the reemergence of psychedelic research. After hearing that Jobs had been influenced by LSD, he decided to write the computer guru a letter to solicit his assistance in these new efforts:

Dear Mr. Steve Jobs,

Hello from Albert Hofmann. I understand from media accounts that you feel LSD helped you creatively in your development of Apple Computers and your personal spiritual quest. I'm interested in learning more about how LSD was useful to you.

I'm writing now, shortly after my 101st birthday, to request that you support Swiss psychiatrist Dr. Peter Gasser's proposed study of LSD-assisted psychotherapy in subjects with anxiety associated with life-threatening illness. This will become the first LSD-assisted psychotherapy study in over 35 years, and will be sponsored by MAPS.

I hope you will help in the transformation of my problem child into a wonder child.

Sincerely
Albert Hofmann

It is unknown if Jobs ever replied to Hofmann or offered any assistance, but the letter provides a strong testimony to Hubbard's influence, illuminating the crossroads where technology and psychedelics first merged in the 1950s and marking the spot where the good Captain hitched his wires to the tail of the universe.

Afterword

WHO WAS THE REAL ALFRED M. HUBBARD?

One of my main objectives in writing this book was to be as factually and historically accurate as possible. This often proved challenging, as many aspects of Hubbard's life have been mythologized over the years, leading to many falsehoods and inaccuracies. When confronting these stories, I tried to go as deep as possible in my research in order to separate fact from fiction. This was not always an easy task, and in some instances, I was unable to arrive at any verifiable conclusion. So, what is and isn't true when it comes to Hubbard? I doubt that will ever be fully known, but I did my best to investigate some of the more legendary aspects of Hubbard's life and offer what the evidentiary record supports. I don't know if "myth busting" is the correct term, but I felt it was important to show my work, as certain parts of this book fly directly in the face of the more conventionally held versions of Hubbard's life. For instance, many sources maintain that Hubbard worked directly for MK-Ultra. Or that he was involved in the Manhattan Project. Or that he introduced LSD to a pope. But are these true?

In order to investigate these stories, I had to go far below what the surface layer of information suggests and do some deep research mining. I visited the National Archives to see what the federal records had to say about Hubbard and mined through the vast amount of research material available at the Seattle Public Library. Luckily, I had visited these locations and photocopied everything prior to COVID-19. The University of

Washington Special Collections also has some great documents related to the "Whispering Wires" trial, and by luck, a historian friend had xeroxed copies of these papers that I was able to use. As of the writing of this book, everything is still shut down, and I'm not sure what I would have done without these pre-pandemic photocopies. I also relied on a variety of online resources, such as the archived collections of the *Seattle Times* and the *Seattle Post-Intelligencer* offered by the Seattle Public Library.

One of the best resources I stumbled across was a cache of documents related to a background check that the FBI had previously conducted on Hubbard. In October 1966, Hubbard completed an "Application for Pardon After Completion of Sentence" form with the Department of Justice. This was during a time when Hubbard was seeking work with various government contractors but his previous prison record (related to his 1936 bootlegging conviction) was negatively affecting his employment prospects. As a result, he sought to have the proverbial slate wiped clean in the form of an official pardon. This prompted the FBI to conduct a background investigation on Hubbard to make sure that he had remained on the legal side of things since his release from prison, as well as to get a general assessment about his current character—the types of factors that a pardon board would need to know and take into consideration when making its decision. The subsequent investigation resulted in a treasure-trove of information about Hubbard. Sometime in 2016, an unknown person submitted a Freedom of Information Act request and was able to obtain these documents. Certain parts were, of course, redacted, but a lot of crucial details were left intact, and the entire trove is available to view online. These documents were important in helping to factually resolve many of the more perplexing aspects of Hubbard's life.

Lastly, I had the good fortune of establishing contact with Hubbard's granddaughter, who generously provided me an unbelievable number of personal insights and background information regarding her legendary grandfather. This was invaluable.

I am, therefore, using this section to break down some of the more sensational and mysterious elements of Hubbard's life and discuss what is and isn't supported. I begin with one of the biggest riddles in Hubbard's life.

WHAT IS THE TRUTH BEHIND THE ATMOSPHERIC POWER GENERATOR?

Probably the biggest mystery surrounding Hubbard was his famous invention, the "atmospheric power generator." So much has been built up about this device over the past one hundred years that it has almost taken on a life all its own. There has long been debate about its legitimacy and what actually powered it. Strangely, there is evidence to support almost all possible scenarios.

Here's what we know about Hubbard's famous generator: it was allegedly a fuelless generator that Hubbard first introduced in December 1919. It was described by eyewitnesses as being a coil-style conductor, eleven inches in diameter and fourteen inches in length, and as Hubbard explained, it was "made up of a group of eight electro-magnets, each with primary and secondary windings of copper wire, which are arranged around a large steel core." Hubbard originally claimed that his device extracted energy from the atmosphere and could be used to power cars, boats and even an entire house. He later retracted these claims in 1928, when an inventor from Pittsburgh had reportedly introduced a machine that was very similar to the atmospheric power generator, and Hubbard was interviewed by the *Seattle Post-Intelligencer* for comment on the story. As Hubbard explained, his generator actually extracted electrical energy from radium, and his original claim was merely subterfuge to protect his patent rights. Strangely, there is no record of such a device with the U.S. Patent Office, though Hubbard was granted a patent for a polonium-tipped spark plug in 1929.

We know that there were three public demonstrations of his device. The first demonstration occurred on December 16, 1919, when Hubbard used his device to power a lightbulb in front of reporters from the *Seattle Post-Intelligencer*. Next came his demonstration on July 28, 1920, when he famously used his generator to power a boat on Lake Union in front of a large crowd of excited spectators. The last known demonstration of his machine occurred on September 17, 1920, when he powered a car for a small gaggle of local reporters in the town of Everett. Aside from this, Hubbard was known to be extremely secretive and protective of his device, and there is only one known instance where he granted a personal inspection. This was, of course, when a professor from a local university examined the generator in 1920 and gave a glowing review about it to the local media.

Afterward, there were no further sightings of the device, though Hubbard incorporated the Hubbard Universal Generator Company in April 1921, for which he sought funding from investors with the promise that millions of dollars in dividends would be paid back once the power generator was patented and enjoying widespread success. It is unknown if any investment capital was raised in these efforts, though Hubbard made a sudden move to Pittsburgh in 1922 and reportedly secured a financial deal with a firm known as the Radium Chemical Company. According to Hubbard's claims, the company allegedly agreed to fund the completion of his device for a majority stake once it received a patent. However, this project never reached completion, and Hubbard soon returned to Seattle empty-handed.

This all took place within a three-year time frame, and the atmospheric power generator essentially then disappeared from the public record. From all this, there are three plausible scenarios:

1. Hubbard's claims were true and he actually invented something quite extraordinary.
2. The whole thing was a sham intended to defraud any would-be investors.
3. He was on the verge of engineering an important new form of technology but wasn't able to fully see it through to the end.

In support of the first scenario, let's start with Hubbard's claim that his device was actually powered by some early form of atomic energy. Hubbard's interest in radioactive energy began during his childhood when one of his uncles introduced him to the field of metallurgy. He was also influenced by a magazine article he read about Ernst Leimer, a German engineer who was considered a pioneer in converting radioactive compounds into usable energy. In his teens, he was somehow able to make a move to Pittsburgh, where he was able to talk his way into some form of on-the-job training with an early radium manufacturer. The name of this company is different depending on which version of the story you're following, but most accounts support that it was Standard Chemical Company. The historical record confirms this was, indeed, a legitimate company and that it was located in Pittsburgh. The record also supports that it was the first company to manufacture radium for commercial use. Hubbard reported that this early employment with Standard Chemical Company taught him how to properly handle radioactive compounds and that he was also able to obtain small quantities of radium for his own experiments. All of this lends direct support to Hubbard's claims that his invention was powered by radium. In fact, we know that Hubbard was quite comfortable with radioactive compounds for most of his life and even became a uranium entrepreneur after World War II.

There is also the gushing deposition from Reverend William E. Smith, who was both an ordained clergyman and professor of physics at an esteemed university. Smith was the first and only known person to have been granted permission to inspect Hubbard's generator. After giving the machine a thorough examination, Smith had this to say about it: "I unhesitatingly say that Hubbard's invention is destined to take the place of existing power generators and that within a few years it will have advanced the whole theory and practice of electricity beyond the dreams of present-day scientists." Strong testimony from a well-respected professor!

From all this, it therefore seems plausible that Hubbard had the knowledge, experience and materials needed to have engineered an early atomic energy device that was capable of generating some amount of electricity, however small that amount may have been.

Later events would also lend support to this. In the 1984 book *The Awesome Life Force*, Joseph H. Cater proposed that Hubbard's device not only worked but that it was one of the most overlooked inventions of the twentieth century. According to Cater's claims, he supposedly built his own working version of Hubbard's atmospheric power generator, though this has never been substantiated or verified.

Oddly, around the same time as the publication of Cater's book, two Seattle engineers published a newsletter article in which they reported that, after years of research and development, they had created an actual working model of Hubbard's generator. They were careful to clarify that the version they created produced only a very small amount of energy but that it proved that the scientific principles of his machine were, in fact, legitimate.

Lastly, when it came to early atomic technology, it should be remembered that Hubbard somewhat proved his scientific merit when U.S. Patent 1,723,422 was issued to him in 1929 for an "internal combustion engine spark plug" modified with radioactive polonium.

On the opposite side of the spectrum, there is also a wide body of evidence that supports the possibility that the atmospheric power generator was a fraudulent contraption. Starting at the beginning of this saga, we know that, despite being very secretive about his device and not allowing anyone to inspect it, Hubbard was fairly quick to solicit funding from would-be investors with his Hubbard Universal Generator Company. It's unknown if he was able to raise any venture capital for his engine, but we do know that several would-be investors were quite skeptical about the

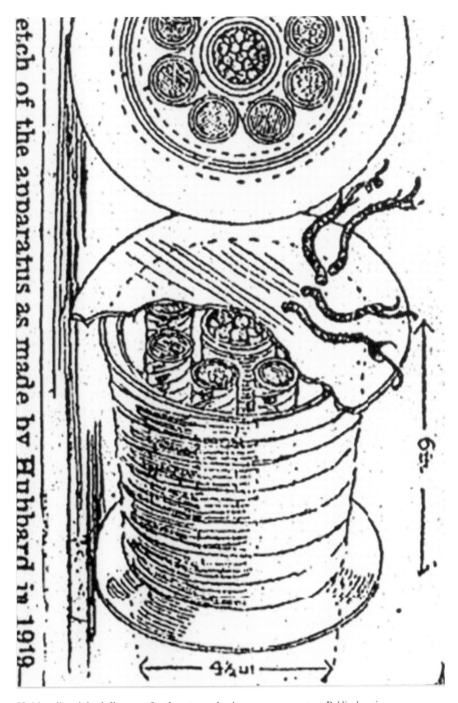

Hubbard's original diagram for the atmospheric power generator. *Public domain.*

whole thing, including the one he allowed to join him on the Lake Union boat demonstration. Even the dean of engineering at the University of Washington was quite public in his skepticism.

There is also the strange matter of Reverend William E. Smith. Despite his original praise of Hubbard's invention, he would later offer a much different testimony. The beginning of this odd chapter starts in 1948, when Hubbard attempted to obtain some uranium from the United States while living in Vancouver, British Columbia. This was immediately following World War II, when atomic energy had suddenly become a very serious matter with high levels of security protocols in place. Hubbard's request for uranium therefore set off alarm bells at the highest levels, prompting an investigation by the Atomic Energy Control Board (AECB), a Canadian governmental agency in charge of regulating nuclear energy. It wanted to know who this Hubbard fellow was and why he was requesting something with such dangerous capabilities. An investigator was quickly dispatched to look into the matter, and he immediately set up an interview with Hubbard himself. Hubbard explained that he had set up a radium business and cited his longtime experience with radioactive energy. During their conversation, Hubbard brought up the atmospheric power generator as an example of his atomic energy experience, during which he mentioned Reverend Smith's testimony. Intrigued, the AECB inspector set up an interview with the physics professor in order to corroborate Hubbard's claims. During the subsequent interview, conducted on May 5, 1948, Smith emphatically claimed the generator was nothing more than "flim flam" and characterized Hubbard as a "bunco man." Without elaborating, Smith claimed that he had been "victimized" into giving false testimony about Hubbard's generator, which he described as a "very crude mechanical contrivance" and further emphasized that it was all a "big fraud." Reverend Smith wasn't able to provide many details to back up these shocking new claims, stating that his memory wasn't completely clear on certain details due to the amount of time that had elapsed since his initial inspection of the device nearly three decades earlier.

The AECB investigator ultimately concluded that Hubbard either had a concealed power source that he used to power the atmospheric power generator or that he had "discovered an entirely new physical phenomenon to this date unknown to 'orthodox' science." The investigator added that he was very reluctant to believe the latter scenario, as it flew in the face of most established science. Largely fueling his skepticism was Hubbard's claim that he had used radium to power his engine, which the investigator dismissed as a scientific impossibility given that radium wasn't known to have any energy-producing properties. Summarizing his impression of Hubbard, he wrote, "There is no doubt in my mind that he is a clever promoter and a rugged individualist who, through his own efforts, rose from very humble beginnings into considerable wealth." The investigator typed up his findings into an official report, and rather curiously, it can be found among the trove of FBI documents from the 1960s.

In 1956, another curious piece of the puzzle was submitted in the form of an article written by Gaston Burridge for *Fate Magazine*, titled "The Hubbard Energy Transformer." Burridge had decided to look into the facts surrounding the atmospheric power generator after having a discussion about such technology with one of his scientific colleagues. The article cites Hubbard's 1929 newspaper interview, in which he revealed that his generator was actually powered by radium. In that same interview, Hubbard also detailed his employment with Radium Chemical Company in Pittsburgh, with which he allegedly worked in order to help develop his device to the point where it would be eligible for a patent. As the story goes, Hubbard reportedly sold the company the rights to his device in the early 1920s, at which point he returned to Seattle and began working on radio technology. Wanting to further look into this matter, Burridge reached out to Radium Chemical Company (which was still in business at the time) and received a reply that none of the employees presently with the company—some of whom worked there in the early 1920s—could remember anything about the device or about Hubbard himself. They added, "There is no information available on the device you mention." Running into a series of similar investigative dead ends, Burridge was never able to reach any substantial conclusions about the legitimacy of the atmospheric power generator and ultimately threw cold water on the possibility that such technology could have existed back then.

One of the most incriminating things to ever surface was a *Seattle Times* article from 1968 titled "Invention Had Everyone Guessing." The author of the article was a local journalist named Ross Cunningham who explained that he had befriended Hubbard when working as a crime reporter during the Prohibition era in the 1920s. He described Hubbard as a "wizard" with a "perpetual and disarming grin." In the article's astonishing claims, Cunningham states that Hubbard had confessed to him that the boat used on the Lake Union demonstration had actually been powered by underwater cables that "pirated" electricity from nearby transmission lines and that Hubbard kept the boat close to shore for these reasons.

Overall, it is very easy to jump to certain conclusions about this mysterious device based on what piece of historical evidence you're looking at. The fact of the matter is, though, that we simply don't know what exactly it was or if there was any degree of legitimacy to it. Perhaps the original model of Hubbard's invention will be uncovered in someone's attic one day, and the matter can finally be resolved once and for all. My own speculation is that Hubbard either created something with unique technological potential or was on the verge of such a breakthrough but, for whatever reason, was never able to see it through to the end. The evidence seems to support that he took a "fake it until you make it" approach to promoting his device and that the early versions of the atmospheric power generator—the versions used to power the light bulb, boat and car—were likely decoys that relied on a hidden power source. It is quite possible that his original generator was able to use an unknown radioactive material to generate electricity, but probably only a very small amount. Perhaps his logic was that, with the right amount of tinkering, he could eventually increase the amount of power being generated, and until he achieved that, he was confident enough in its promise that he made the decision to promote it anyway. At some point, though, he probably realized he was in over his head and decided to abandon ship. While this may sound like justification for some of Hubbard's more dishonorable deeds, I feel that it's the scenario with the best evidentiary support.

Having said that, there are still a lot of unresolved questions and mysterious footnotes to this whole story that I don't think will ever be satisfactorily resolved. One of the biggest for me was Reverend Smith's original testimony and his later dramatic reversal. Why did a well-respected physics professor (and ordained clergyman) from a very esteemed university risk his reputation, and possibly even his career, on making such a false claim? Was he coerced or intimidated into this somehow, as he claimed in 1948? And if so, by whom? Hubbard wasn't ever known to have physically intimidated or bullied anyone. Was Hubbard's father, William, the person behind the threats?

Also, who did Hubbard really work for in Pittsburgh? The record indicates that he spent two different periods of time in Pittsburgh. During the first stint, from 1916 through 1917, Hubbard allegedly talked his way into a job with Standard Chemical Company, where he learned the fundamentals of atomic energy. Hubbard then returned to Pittsburgh in 1921 and reportedly negotiated a business agreement with the Radium Chemical Company to help get his invention patented. Curiously, there is

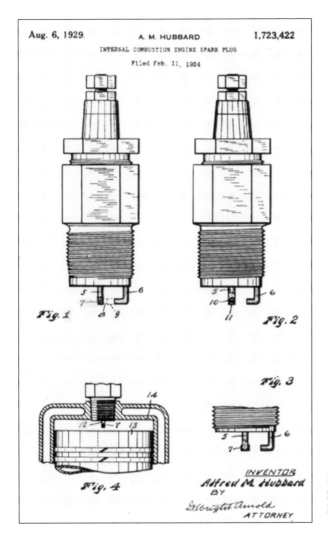

Diagram for Hubbard's polonium-tipped spark plug that he patented in 1929. *Public domain.*

an established connection between the two companies. Records show that Standard Chemical Company—the first commercial producer of radium—was owned by a man by the name of Joseph Flannery, who also owned the Flannery Bolt Company, which operated out of the same building as Hubbard's second employer, the Radium Chemical Company. Even more mysteriously, there was a physicist at the Flannery Bolt Company by the name of Grover R. Greenslade who developed inventions very similar to some of Hubbard's. Specifically, in May 1922, Greenslade filed U.S. Patent No. 1,523,013 for a device that used polonium to create a conductive path between spaced electrical conductors. The patent was granted to him in

1925. This sounds very similar to Hubbard's polonium-tipped spark plug, and it is on record that the two men knew each other. Hubbard mentioned Greenslade by name in a newspaper interview, in which he reported that Greenslade "represented people who were financing me at the time." From all this, we know that these Pittsburgh atomic energy companies were all somehow interrelated and involved a physicist who developed inventions very similar to Hubbard's. This, then, begs the question: were Hubbard's inventions inspired by Greenslade, or was Greenslade inspired by Hubbard? And whatever happened to the atmospheric power generator? If Radium Chemical Company purchased the rights to Hubbard's engine, as was reported, then why was it never patented?

Curiously, the answer to that last question may lie in the strange saga of a man by the name of Lester J. Hendershot, an engineer who reportedly developed a fuelless motor very similar to the atmospheric power generator. In 1928, the Hendershot Generator had its first public demonstration at a Detroit airfield when it was used to power a large model airplane. The event was intended to showcase a new technology that could also be used to fly regular aircraft. Among those in the crowd that day was famous aviator Charles Lindbergh. The *Seattle Post-Intelligencer* reached out to Hubbard in order to get a comment on the similarities between his invention and the one that had just been showcased in Detroit. It was during this interview that Hubbard made the claim that his device had actually been powered by radium, prompting him to elaborate on his involvement with Radium Chemical Company, which he suggested was now introducing his ideas as its own through Hendershot. Indeed, records corroborate that Hendershot's town of residence was Pittsburgh, not too far from the site of the company's headquarters. When Hendershot was asked how his generator operated, he explained that it worked by "using the Earth's magnetic fields to generate rotary motion." This was very similar to Hubbard's original explanation of the atmospheric power generator, when he stated that it "transformed the earth's line of magnetic forces into electrical energy available for use." Is it therefore possible that Radium Chemical Company stole Hubbard's ideas and used Hendershot as a front? Sadly, the answer to that question will likely never be satisfactorily answered, as Hendershot would later die of a very suspicious suicide after claiming that various corporate and political entities had been actively trying to halt any further development of his invention. There are no straightforward conclusions to be drawn from any of this, but these strange series of events and mysterious connections certainly sound like the ingredients of a juicy conspiracy theory.

Overall, the atmospheric power generator is one of the most perplexing enigmas surrounding Hubbard's life, and I personally find some amount of solace in the fact that many questions about it will likely never be answered. It keeps things interesting, and after all, not all mysteries need to be solved.

DID HUBBARD WORK AS A TAXI DRIVER DURING PROHIBITION AND INSTALL A RADAR IN HIS TRUNK?

According to this particular storyline, Hubbard worked as a taxi driver during Prohibition, but the job was actually a clever front for certain bootlegging operations. As the story goes, Hubbard kept a radar in the trunk of the cab that was used to assist Olmstead's fleet of ships and help them avoid capture by the Coast Guard. The origins of this story are unknown, but I found no evidence that mentioned Hubbard ever working as a taxi driver. Also, Hubbard was quite skilled when it came to radio communications equipment, but there are no known instances of him ever working with any type of radar technology. Not to mention, it seems extremely unlikely that a 1920s radar could even fit in the trunk of a car. Therefore, due to a complete lack of any evidentiary support, this particular story appears to be false.

WAS HUBBARD RELATED IN ANY WAY TO SCIENTOLOGY FOUNDER L. RON HUBBARD?

There are no known family relations between the two men. I even spoke to a man who had posted his family genealogy project online and whose expansive family tree included Hubbard. His research concluded that there was no connection between Hubbard's bloodline and the famous Scientologist. As far as the evidence goes, there's nothing to suggest any type of relation or that they even knew each other. So, this can also be verified as false.

WAS HUBBARD REALLY INVOLVED IN A SECRET WORLD WAR II OPERATION?

All historical evidence seems to support that Hubbard was at least peripherally involved in a World War II operation known as the Lend-Lease Program. This operation, authorized by Franklin D. Roosevelt on January 10, 1941, provided military aid to various Allied war countries, including Russia and Great Britain. The United States had not yet formally entered the war, so the plan was intended to help beat back Hitler's advances while still technically remaining a neutral country. According to the conventional storyline, Hubbard was approached by the OSS in 1941 and asked to participate in a top-secret war operation where ships and planes were smuggled to Canada and then sent to England to be used in the war effort. As mentioned in a previous chapter, the OSS wasn't formally established until June 13, 1942, which was a year after the Land-Lease Program began. Likely, Hubbard would have been approached by U.S. Naval intelligence. In fact, records show that Hubbard's ship at the time, the SS *Machigonne*, was acquired by the U.S. Navy in February 1941, thus supporting that he had been in some form of contact with navy officials when all of this supposedly began.

As far as the operation itself, the ships and planes would have been sent to Russia, not England, as part of the Northwest Staging Route—a string of Canadian airfields leading through what is now Alaska and into Soviet territory. Typically, American planes would be covertly flown up to Vancouver and, from there, up to Alberta, over to Alaska and finally over to Russia to be used against the German invasion. So, Hubbard's involvement likely involved the first stage of this operation where vessels were smuggled from Washington State up to British Columbia. He certainly would have been a good candidate for such a mission given his excellent knowledge of Pacific Northwest smuggling routes, his proficiency in radio communications and his skills in being able to operate in a covert manner.

Hubbard's involvement is further corroborated by evidence found in the FBI documents. When Hubbard was interviewed by the AECB in 1948, he reported that he made good money buying ships in the United States and then sailing them into Canadian ports to be "seized" by Canadian authorities, who then compensated him for these efforts. Later, in the paperwork completed for his pardon request in 1966, he listed that he was the "Director of Engineering" at Marine Sales and Services in Vancouver, British Columbia, from 1941 through 1947. In parenthesis, it is noted that "applicant stated that this company was part of the Canadian External Affairs Department and handled military items sent to Canada by the U.S." We also know that Hubbard was suddenly quite wealthy after the war and that he was successfully able to start a uranium business, which only seems possible if he had access to key and influential people.

It therefore seems very likely that Hubbard was involved in the Lend-Lease Program on some level, though it is unknown if Hubbard worked directly with the U.S. government on this or if he somehow found his own backdoor way into making money from the operation.

WHAT WAS HUBBARD'S INVOLVEMENT WITH THE MANHATTAN PROJECT?

This ties directly into Hubbard's involvement in the Lend-Lease Program, as certain accounts of his life say that he was involved in the Manhattan Project—a very covert top-secret operation during World War II that produced the atomic weapons used in the bombings of Hiroshima and Nagasaki, Japan.

The primary source of this story appears to have been a 1980 article for *Vancouver* magazine in which the author, Ben Metcalfe, claimed that Hubbard had once shown him "photographs of himself accompanying the American-Canadian party into Port Radium to pick up the first shipment of uranium for the Manhattan Project." Port Radium is a mining area on the eastern shore of Great Bear Lake in the Northwest Territories of Canada, and quite fittingly, Port Radium has been historically mined for radium and uranium. In fact, during World War II, over 10 percent of all uranium used in the Manhattan Project came from Port Radium.

The company tasked with mining uranium at Port Radium was an outfit known as Eldorado Crown Resources. Interestingly, when interviewed in 1948, Hubbard told the AECB investigator that he was in negotiations with the Eldorado Crown Resources Company to become its agent for radium sales. So, there is fairly good evidence supporting that Hubbard had business ties to the mining company directly responsible for providing a significant amount of uranium to the Manhattan Project.

Could Hubbard's trip to Port Radium have been somehow connected to the Lend-Lease Program? A side assignment he was given, perhaps? The timing of everything would certainly fit with this hypothesis. Unfortunately, there are no "smoking gun" documents that can verify anything, so the truth will likely never be known. But a lot of different parts of this story seem to fit together rather nicely, so it seems quite plausible that Hubbard was at least peripherally involved in the infamous Manhattan Project.

DID HUBBARD TURN A POPE ON TO LSD?

One of the more fantastical stories about Hubbard was that he actually turned one of the popes on to LSD. This seems unlikely just on its face, and there is no evidence to support that it ever happened. The likely origin of this rumor was Timothy Leary's claim that Hubbard knew the pope, who at the time of their meeting would have been Pope Paul VI. We also know that Hubbard introduced LSD to the priest of a Vancouver church in the 1950s. Likely, these two storylines converged at some point, resulting in the myth that Hubbard had given LSD to one of the popes.

WAS HUBBARD INVOLVED IN MK-ULTRA?

One of the more long-standing rumors about Hubbard was that he was somehow involved in MK-Ultra, the infamous experiments beginning in the 1950s when the CIA dosed unsuspecting people with LSD in the interest of learning how psychedelics could possibly be weaponized. Despite Hubbard's denial of such claims, stories about his involvement are persistent, and there are several details that lend support to the idea that he may have had some degree of involvement.

Probably the biggest culprit behind the MK-Ultra rumors was Hubbard's long-term involvement with various government entities. Starting in the Prohibition days, when Hubbard worked covertly as a Prohibition agent for the U.S. Treasury Department, and on through World War II, when he allegedly participated in top-secret military operations on behalf of the OSS, there is no shortage of Hubbard's connections to various deep state operations within the U.S. government. His World War II work in particular stands out, as the OSS was the precursor to the CIA, which was, of course, the agency that carried out MK-Ultra. So, it's very easy to play a game of connect-the-dots and arrive at the conclusion that the "Johnny Appleseed of LSD" could likely have had a hand in such things.

There is also his mysterious employment at Teledyne from 1964 through 1965. Many accounts from his time there claim that he worked as a "human factors analyst," testing the effects of mind-altering agents on military personnel in order to "develop techniques in areas of military interests." Other sources maintain that Hubbard's employment at Teledyne involved a secret NASA project in which astronauts and pilots were given psychotropic drugs. If true, then there are obvious similarities between this Teledyne work and what the CIA was doing with MK-Ultra.

Lastly, there is Hubbard's work at the Stanford Research Institute in the late 1960s and early 1970s. The program was run by one of Hubbard's longtime LSD colleagues, Willis Harman, who described Hubbard's duties at SRI as "gathering various sorts of data regarding student unrest, drug abuse, drug use at schools and universities, causes and nature of radical activities, and similar matters, some of a classified nature." In other words, Hubbard was tasked with spying on the hippie movement, gathering intelligence about their drug and antiwar activities. The exact same time this was going on, the CIA had also become interested in the activities of the 1960s counterculture and shifted much of its focus over to monitoring underground LSD networks and antiwar protests. So once again, there was a direct overlap between Hubbard's job duties at the time and certain objectives of the CIA.

Is it therefore possible that the man who developed LSD therapy and had long-term connections to the U.S. government at its deepest levels could have been involved with a program such as MK-Ultra? Of course. But forcing psychedelics on unwitting test subjects was never Hubbard's modus operandi. There has never been so much as a suggestion that Hubbard was ever duplicitous or deceitful in administering psychotropic drugs to people. In fact, Hubbard held such a sacramental view of psychedelics that he walked away from several lucrative job opportunities when he felt that these substances were being misused or commercialized for financial gain. Lastly, Hubbard went on the record as vehemently denying any involvement with the CIA.

If Hubbard ever offered any type of assistance to the MK-Ultra program, it likely occurred during his employment with SRI when he was actively conducting espionage on the countercultural activities of the New Left. The CIA was conducting parallel operations at the same time, so it's quite possible that there may have been some intel sharing between them.

However, the exact truth of Hubbard's involvement will likely never be known, as most of the records from MK-Ultra were destroyed in 1973 upon orders by then CIA director Richard Helms, who cited the reason as "a paper crisis."

PART OF HUBBARD'S ALLURE rests in many of these stories and, whether true or not, paints a good picture of just what a larger-than-life character he actually was. He was somehow able to cram several lifetimes into one, giving rise to a spectacular mythology. Some of this is supported by the empirical evidence, but not all. In the end, it ultimately doesn't matter if he drove a taxi with a radar in the trunk or dispensed LSD to a pope because, after truth has been sifted from fiction, we are still left with a stunning biography of a man who, despite his many human flaws, led a very remarkable and well-lived life and whose contributions are still shaping the world around us.

SOURCES

Books

Abramson, Harold A. *The Use of LSD in Psychotherapy.* New York: Josiah Macy Jr. Foundation Publications, 1960.

Adler, Gerhard. *C.G. Jung Letters.* Vol. 2, *1951–1961.* London: Routledge & Kegan Paul, 1973.

Albarelli, H.P., Jr. *A Terrible Mistake.* Walterville, OR: TrineDay Press, 2009.

Anderson, Walter Truett. *The Upstart Spring.* Indianapolis, IN: Addison-Wesley Publishing, 1983.

Cater, Joseph H. *The Awesome Life Force.* Clayton, GA: Cadake Industries/Health Research, 1984.

Clarke, Norman H. *The Dry Years: Prohibition and Social Change in Washington.* Seattle: University of Washington Press, 1965.

Dyck, Erika. *Psychedelic Psychiatry: LSD from Clinic to Campus.* Baltimore, MD: Johns Hopkins University Press, 2008.

Dyck, Erika, Cynthia Carson Bisbee, Paul Bisbee, Patrick Farrell, James Sexton and James W. Spisak. *Psychedelic Prophets: The Letters of Aldous Huxley and Humphrey Osmond.* Montreal, Quebec: McGill–Queen's University Press, 2018.

Fry, Peter. *Beyond the Mechanical Mind.* N.p.: ABC Books, 1977.

Hoffman, Albert. *LSD, My Problem Child: Reflections on Sacred Drugs, Mysticism and Science.* Santa Cruz, CA: Multidisciplinary Association for Psychedelic Studies, 1979.

Holden, Brad. *Seattle Prohibition: Bootleggers, Rumrunners & Graft in the Queen City.* Charleston, SC: The History Press, 2019.

Huxley, Aldous. *The Doors of Perception.* London: Pelican Books, 1954.

———. *Moksha.* Los Angeles: Tarcher, 1982.

Lattin, Don. *The Harvard Psychedelic Club: How Timothy Leary, Ram Dass, Huston Smith, and Andrew Weil Killed the Fifties and Ushered in a New Age for America.* San Francisco: HarperOne, 2011.

Leary, Timothy. *Flashbacks: A Personal and Cultural History of an Era.* New York: G.P. Putnam's Sons, 1990.

Leary, Timothy, and James Penner. *Timothy Leary, the Harvard Years: Early Writings on LSD and Psilocybin with Richard Alpert, Huston Smith, Ralph Metzler and Others.* Rochester, VT: Park Street Press, 2014.

Lee, Martin A., and Bruce Shlain. *Acid Dreams: The Complete History of LSD: The CIA, the Sixties and Beyond.* New York: Grove Press, 1985.

Markoff, John. *What the Dormouse Said: How the Sixties Counterculture Shaped the Personal Computing Industry.* New York: Viking Penguin, 2005.

Metcalfe, Phillip. *Whispering Wires: The Tragic Tale of an American Bootlegger.* Portland, OR: Inkwater Press, 2007.

Newsome, Eric. *Pass the Bottle: Rum Tales of the West Coast.* Victoria, BC: Orca Book Publishers, 1995.

Pollan, Michael. *How to Change Your Mind: What the New Science of Psychedelics Teaches Us About Consciousness, Dying, Addiction, Depression and Transcendence.* New York: Random House, 2018.

Stevens, Jay. *Storming Heaven: LSD and the American Dream.* New York: Grove Press, 1998.

Stolaroff, Myron J. *Thanatos to Eros: 35 Years of Psychedelic Exploration.* N.p.: Thaneros Press, 1994.

Wolfe, Tom. *The Electric Kool-Aid Acid Test.* New York: Bantam Books, 1981.

Scientific Essays and Academic Publications

Bleweet, D.B., PhD, and N. Chwelos, MD. "The Handbook of the Therapeutic Use of LSD-25, Individuals and Group Procedure." 1959. (Note: there was no formal publisher for this work; rather, copies were mimeographed by the authors and disseminated throughout the psychedelic underground.)

Cole, Jonathan O., and Martin M. Katz. "The Psychotomimetic Drugs: An Overview." *Journal of the American Medical Association* 10 (1964): 187.

Hubbard, Al, et al. "The Use of LSD-25 in the Treatment of Alcoholism and Other Psychiatric Problems." *Quarterly Journal of Studies on Alcohol* (March 1961).

Oram, Matthew. "Prohibited or Regulated? LSD Psychotherapy and the United States Food and Drug Administration." University of Calgary, Canada, 2016.

Sandison, Ronald A., et al. "Therapeutic Value of Lysergic Acid Diethlyamide in Mental Illness." *Journal of Mental Science* 100, no. 419 (1954).

Sherwood, J.N., MS, M.J. Stolaroff and W.W. Harman, PhD. "The Psychedelic Experience: A New Concept in Psychotherapy." *Journal of Psychedelic Drugs* (April 1968): 96–111.

Smythies, John, and Humphry Osmond. "The Present State of Psychological Medicine." *Hibbert Journal* (1953): 133–42.

Magazines

Burridge, Gaston. "The Hubbard Energy Transformer." *Fate Magazine*, July 1956.

Chandler, Thomas. "LSD Cures the Insane." *Look Magazine*, September 1954.

Fahey, Todd Brendan. "The Original Captain Trips." *High Times Magazine*, November 1991.

Fleming, F.D. "The Hendershot Motor Mystery." *Fate Magazine*, January 1950.

Mecklin, John. "Medicine: The Dream Stuff." *Time*, June 1954.

Metcalfe, Ben. "Doctor Acid: Al Hubbard Brought LSD to New Westminster and the World." *Vancouver Magazine*, September 1980.

Moore, Gerald, and Larry Schiller. "LSD: The Exploding Threat of the Mind Drug That Got Out of Control." *Life*, March 1966.

Wasson, Robert Gordon. "Seeking the Magic Mushroom." *Time*, May 1957.

Newspapers

Carter, Don. "Saga of a Boy Inventor and His Mystery Machine." *Seattle Post-Intelligencer*, July 16, 1973, 1.

Colville Examiner. "A New X-ray Machine Has Been Invented by Alfred M. Hubbard." September 24, 1921, 7.

Cunningham, Ross. "Invention Had Everyone Guessing." *Seattle Times*, August 18, 1968, 26.

Dremman, Sue. "Palo Alto's Magical Mystery Trip." *Palo Alto Weekly*, November 3, 2018.

Leavenworth Echo. "More About Hubbard's Invention." August 6, 1920, 6.

New York Tribune. "Seattle Youth Comes Here with Patents for Device Said to Generate Power from the Atmosphere." October 4, 1920, 11.

Oregon News Review. "Six Out of Nine Convicted in *Zev* Liquor Plot Case." February 27, 1928, 3.

Sacramento Union. "Engineers Wonder as Youth Shows Device He Professes Captures Power of Universe." December 22, 1919.

San Bernardino County Sun. "Five Arrested with $1,000,000 Smuggling Quiz." March 5, 1936, 1.

Seattle Post-Intelligencer. "Alfred M. Hubbard Arrested: U.S. Jails Five Smugglers." March 4, 1936, 11.

———. "Engineers Wonder as Youth Shows Device He Professes Captures Power of Universe." December 16, 1919, 1.

———. "Fired by Jones, Says Hubbard." November 22, 1932, 5.

———. "Hubbard Believes Mystery Motor Based on His Own Invention." February 27, 1928, 2.

———. "Hubbard Coil Runs Boat on Portage Bay at Ten Knots an Hour; Auto Test Next." July 29, 1920, 1.

———. "Hubbard Key Figure in Rum Case." October 17, 1927, 1.

———. "Hubbard Protects His Coil." August 6, 1920, 1.

———. "'Hubbard's New Energy Device No Fake,' Says Seattle College Man." December 17, 1919, 1.

———. "Olmstead Quiz Featured by Mysterious Radio." November 3, 1929, 39.

———. "Undercover Agent Wasn't Well Hidden." August 28, 1930, 2.

———. "U.S. Suspends Two Agents." September 10, 1927, 1.

———. "Whitney Alarmed, Joined Rum Ring, Says Hubbard." August 16, 1930, 2.

Seattle Star. "Boy Inventor May Give Demonstration." December 19, 1919, 10.

———. "Demonstration of Boy's Invention Is Being Planned." December 18, 1919, 4.

———. "Electricity of Air Runs Boat." July 29, 1920, 7.

———. "Hubbard and His Invention." December 22, 1919, 6.

———. "Mystery Generator Is Hooked to Auto." August 24, 1920, 3.

———. "Professor Permitted to Study Youth's Discovery." December 17, 1919, 9.

Seattle Times. "Al Hubbard Aids Agents in $30,000 Booze Raid." December 6, 1931, 1.

———. "Al Hubbard in L.A. Rum Quiz." March 4, 1936, 2.

———. "Appeal in Zev Case Lost in High Court." December 10, 1928, 5.

———. "Booze, Bribes, Radio Covered by Witness During First Day Quiz." August 22, 1930, 8.

———. "'Boy Inventor' Answers Charges He Was Coerced into Signing Contract." October 26, 1923, 7.

———. "Daily Marriage Licenses." August 29, 1920, 15.

———. "Fists Fly at Al Hubbard After Verdict; 14 Guilty." October 23, 1927, 1.

———. "Former Aide to Olmsted [sic] Turned Spy After Raid." May 19, 1926, 1.

———. "Former Dry Convicted of Mexican Smuggling." September 22, 1936, 1.

———. "Four Local Stations Are Deleted." April 6, 1925, 10.

———. "Hubbard Is Revealed as Secret Aide of Whitney." May 16, 1926, 1.

———. "Hubbard, Roy Olmstead's Friend, Sued for Divorce." September 10, 1926, 9.

———. "Hubbard Tells of Dry Trap." May 2, 1927, 11.

———. "Parker Nabs 'Booze King' on His Own Accusation." November 29, 1925, 1.

———. "U.S. Agents Seize 111 Cases of Booze Near Des Moines." November 26, 1925, 1.

———. "Who's Who in Indictments." January 20, 1925, 1.

Slater, Laura. "How Psychedelic Drugs Can Help Patients Face Death." New York Times, April 20, 2012.

Spokane Chronicle. "Generator Trust Wins Court O.K." August 4, 1921, 3.

———. "Juice from Air to Be Financed." June 27, 1921, 3.

———. "Jury Exonerates Prohibition Men." March 23, 1928, 11.

———. "Law Enforcers Hire Bootlegger." December 28, 1926, 13.

———. "Ryan Testifies Legal Advisor Out to 'Get' Rum Ring." August 27, 1930, 1.

———. "U.S. Ex-Attorney on Stand at Trial of Roy Lyle." September 10, 1930, 1.

———. "X-Ray Machine Invented Here." September 20, 1921, 1.

Spokesman-Review. "Lyle Defense Hits Hard in First Broadside." August 15, 1930, 1.

Swisher, Kara. "How and Why Silicon Valley Gets High." *New York Times,* August 23, 2018.

Vancouver Sun. "B.C.'s Acid Flashback." December 8, 2001, 15.

Washington Herald. "Boy Inventor Drives Boat with Mysterious Electric Air Engine—Experts Scoff." August 30, 1920, 2.

Washington Standard. "Hubbard Universal Generator Company Files Incorporation." April 22, 1921, 1.

Historical Archives

Bureau of Prohibition Files, National Archives—Pacific Northwest Region. Record Group 56, Box 1 (folders 3.01-237), Box 2 (folder 28S-70S), Box 3 (folder 97S-99S), Box 5–6, Box 20 (folder 1055M), Box 31 (folder 2440M). Department of the Treasury, Seattle, WA.

The Charles Gates Papers. Accession No: 0364-001, Box 24, folder 1, Roy Olmstead, Rumrunning King of the Pacific Northwest. UW Special Collections, University of Washington, Seattle, WA.

The Charles Moriarty Sr. Papers. Accession No: 3009-001, Box 7, folders 2-14, CASE FILES—U.S. vs. Whitney, et al., U.S. Opening Statement: Savage Address to the Jury: Moriarty. UW Special Collections, University of Washington, Seattle, WA.

Marino v. United States, 91 F.2d 691 (1937) No. 8343. Circuit Court of Appeals, Ninth Circuit. July 28, 1937.

Online

"Documents on Al Hubbard." The Memory Hole, www.thememoryhole. org/hubbard.

Erowid. www.erowid.org.

"League Island (YFB 20) ex–USS *Machigonne.*" www.navsource.org/ archives/12/171043.htm.

"Radioactive Spark Plugs." www.orau.org/ptp/collection/consumer%20 products/sparkplugs.htm.

Unarium Wisdom. www.unariumwisdom.com/wp-content/uploads/2020/07/ Hubbard-Coil-Generator.

USDJ/FBI report no. 73-15666, dated February 10, 1967. The Archive, www.archive.org/details/AlHubbard/page/n15.

Podcasts

Psychedelic Salon Podcast. Episode 83, interview with Jean and Myron Stolaroff, March 15, 2007. www.psychedelicsalon.com.

Author Interview

Interviews with Brooke Hart (Al Hubbard's granddaughter), March 2020–February 2021.

ABOUT THE AUTHOR

Photo by Jim Hamerlinck.

Brad Holden is an author, historian and "finder of old things." When not out searching for local historical artifacts, he enjoys writing about Seattle's past. His work has appeared in *Pacific Northwest Magazine*, and he is a contributing writer for HistoryLink.org, an online encyclopedia of Washington State history. Holden has been profiled in *Seattle Magazine*, *Seattle Refined* and various regional newspapers. His previous book, *Seattle Prohibition: Bootleggers, Rumrunners & Graft in the Queen City*, was released to much critical acclaim in 2019. He lives in Edmonds, Washington.

Visit us at
www.historypress.com